Whose Church?

Also by Daniel C. Maguire

The Horrors We Bless:
Rethinking the Just-War Legacy

A Moral Creed for All Christians

Sacred Rights:
The Case for Contraception and Abortion
in World Religions

What Men Owe to Women:
Men's Voices from World Religions

Ethics for a Small Planet:
New Horizons on Population, Consumption,
and Ecology

Whose Church?

A CONCISE GUIDE TO

PROGRESSIVE CATHOLICISM

Daniel C. Maguire

THE NEW PRESS

NEW YORK
LONDON

Requests for permission to reproduce selections from this book should be
mailed to: Permissions Department, The New Press, 38 Greene Street,
New York, NY 10013.

Published in the United States by The New Press, New York, 2008
Distributed by W. W. Norton & Company, Inc., New York

LIBRARY OF CONGRESS CATALOGING-IN-PUBLICATION DATA

Maguire, Daniel C.
Whose church? : a concise guide to progressive Catholicism /
Daniel C. Maguire.
    p.   cm.
Includes bibliographical references.
ISBN 978-1-59558-335-2 (hc.)
1. Liberalism.   2. Catholic Church—History—21st century.   I. Title.
BX1396.2.M34   2007
282.09'51—dc22   2007045961

The New Press was established in 1990 as a not-for-profit alternative to the
large, commercial publishing houses currently dominating the book
publishing industry. The New Press operates in the public interest rather
than for private gain, and is committed to publishing, in innovative ways,
works of educational, cultural, and community value that are often deemed
insufficiently profitable.

www.thenewpress.com

Composition by dix!
This book was set in New Caledonia

Printed in the United States of America

2   4   6   8   10   9   7   5   3   1

*To Edie McFadden, my wife, "a heart
that laughter has made sweet"
(W. B. Yeats)*

Contents

Foreword

Daniel Maguire is among the most important Roman Catholic social ethicists writing today. He has never hesitated to expose his church's most unjust, life-denying teachings with both a sense of humor and a sensitivity to tragedy. He has, more importantly, spent his career drawing out the best in Catholic ethics. He writes with an appreciation for the ethical dilemmas ordinary people face and with acute antennae for the ridiculous.

The New Press is committed to bringing the best progressive voices in religion to a wide public. Those who appreciate clear vision and thinking about the best in Catholicism will be grateful to find so much in one volume. *Whose Church?* offers readers perceptive insights on six crucial issues maligned or neglected by the religious right: sexuality, war and peace, poverty and economic justice, the rights of women, race, and the environment. The current pope, Benedict, knows Maguire's work well, though it would be safe to say he does not regard it with affection.

Maguire is also well known among American bishops. Rev. Thomas G. Weinandy, executive director of the U.S.

Conference of Catholic Bishops' doctrine committee, said it was "quite unusual" for them to denounce Catholic theologians formally, especially when the Vatican had not issued something first. However, according to a March 23, 2007, story in the *New York Times,* the U.S. bishops took such an unusual step by condemning Maguire's teaching on contraception, abortion, and gay marriage. As grounds for this preemptory move, Father Weinandy noted that Maguire's pamphlets were "written in a very popular and lively style, and from what the bishops knew, they were very widely distributed." News of this action resulted in at least one Web site in Italy posting a Maguire brochure on gay marriage, translated into Italian.

Trained at Rome's prestigious Pontifical Gregorian University, Maguire began his career as a priest. He went on to become a noted scholar and teacher. In his work as a professional theologian, he has not hesitated to criticize official church teachings, to offer an alternative grounded in solid Catholic thinkers, and to defend colleagues engaged in similar reform of the Church. In April 1967, when the board of trustees of the Catholic University of America voted to deny a unanimous recommendation by the academic senate that Professor Charles Curran be reappointed and promoted, Maguire and colleagues at the institution's School of Theology led a nearly weeklong strike by faculty and students that shut down the entire university. The board rescinded its decision.

Curran's published works, according to then–Cardinal Ratzinger, contained "principal errors" from traditional Catholic dogma on abortion, contraception, and homosexuality. Maguire and Curran would later receive support and awards from progressive Catholics for their courage in defending progressive ideas as true Catholic teaching.

Maguire has continued to make strategic interventions on major social issues. His work prompted *Ms.* magazine in 1982 to vote him among "40 male heroes of the past decade, men who took chances and made a difference." The students of the University of Notre Dame selected him in 1983–84 as one of the ten top teachers. In 2001, when the Vatican attempted to require Catholic professors to receive a mandate from their bishops, Maguire refused. He noted that the ruling violated the academic freedom of American universities and would subject trained theologians to the judgment of those who are not professional theologians, putting the bishops into the indefensible position of judging scholars without the benefit of the appropriate expertise. Maguire did not think reliance on divine assistance was an adequate substitute for intellectual training and years of study.

While American Protestant Christians tend to rely far more on the biblical text, on faith, and on personal experience, Roman Catholics have, in addition, nearly two millennia of sophisticated ethical reflection by the best thinkers of their times. This body of teaching has had a profound impact on social teaching and law in Western secular society as well as in the Church. Maguire does not hesitate to dismantle the problematic aspects of that tradition. He also notes what it continues to offer as a reflection on human moral behavior. This twofold process of critique and retrieval brings renewal and credibility to progressive Catholicism on such issues as war, poverty, and—surprising to some—sex, and this work offers ethical resources to those who seek spiritual options beyond crass consumerist secularism and rigid, narrow religion.

Maguire's lifelong commitment to progressive religious ideas, distilled in the pages of this book, could not come to the American public at a more important moment in this young century. The ascendancy of the political religious right and the disgraceful meddling of conservative Catholic leaders in the 2004 national election have left many with the impression that "pelvic issues"—Maguire's apt term—dominate Roman Catholic ethics. In the wake of sexual abuse scandals, the Vatican has chosen homophobic purges and retrenchment into ever more conservative teaching.

In this book we hear views for the neglected Catholic majority, the faithful who have been abandoned by their leaders. Maguire offers social teaching for all who care about the poor, about the oppressed, about ending war, about reproductive rights, about the environment, and about good sex—those who seek to live out the best in Catholic social teachings and their many progressive friends and allies.

Rita Nakashima Brock
Series Editor

Whose Church?

Introduction

Left-wingers, bow low to your masters and doff your hats to right-wingers. They are without equal in the art of hijacking religious power and subverting it to their own purposes. Sometimes, as in the USA, they even commandeer a political party in the process. Skill is skill and should be acknowledged.

There is an old Russian saying: "Fear has big eyes." Right-wingers are scared, hyperventilating people—scared of other nations, other classes, other races, other genders, other sexual orientations—and so their eyes are big and focused. They know that in politics, power wins. And they know that religions are powerhouses pumping energy into the public square, defining everything from what counts as "moral values" or "family values" to how good people should vote. They even throw in religiously disguised meat to pump up "the dogs of war."

Power-hungry politicians drape themselves in pious rhetoric. God talk rises in proportion to the mischief afoot.

John Henry Cardinal Newman put it this way: People will die for a dogma who will not stir for a conclusion. Camus added that people will not die for scientific truth. Joining the chorus on the power of religion from the underside, the poet Alexander Pope said that the worst of madmen is a saint gone mad. Even Sam Harris, the reigning hammer of all things religious, believes that religion has the power to "determine our future."[1]

For good or for ill, nothing so stirs the human will as the tincture of the sacred, and those who do not know that are sociologically naive.[2] As Huston Smith says: "Wherever religion comes to life it displays a startling quality; it takes over. All else, while not silenced, becomes subdued and thrown without contest into a supporting role."[3]

Lazy left-wingers are the great enablers, carelessly basking in the illusion that the First Amendment and the intentionally Godless Constitution removed religion from American life. Meanwhile, closer to the street, Theocracy USA blooms around them and suffuses American politics and policies.

American "sophisticates" willingly credit the power of religion to produce horrors, like witch hunts, inquisitions, and pogroms, but that is too simple. As Garry Wills writes, most of the good revolutionary movements that transformed, shaped, and reshaped the American nation—"abolitionism, women's suffrage, the union movement, the civil rights movement— . . . grew out of religious circles."[4] Religion can go either way, but it is always going.

Reeling from centuries of what Edward Luttwak calls "religiously contrived ignorance," eighteenth-century Enlightenment thinkers effectively excommunicated the study of religious influence on secular affairs. "Enlightenment publicists and philosophers wielded none of the torture instruments of the Catholic inquisitions, nor did they burn dissenters under some Protestant dispensation. But when it came to religion in all its aspects, they strangled free inquiry just as effectively," denying respectability to the serious study of religious social power.[5] A revealingly entitled study from the Oxford University Press, *Religion: The Missing Dimension of Statecraft*, shows how decision after decision in U.S. foreign policy was bungled and bewitched by the failure to take religion seriously as an active agent in a whole series of international crises. This studied ignorance sits atop our policies toward Iraq, Iran, and Israel.

Actually, it is here, in foreign affairs, that the right and the left unite in a Coalition of the Stupid. Recent history shows that though the American right wing is shrewder in seeing the power of religion domestically, both right and left miss the religious muscle operating in national and international affairs.

IRONY OF IRONIES

Now here's a zinger. The world's religions are left-wing movements. It's hard to imagine Jesus or his mother, or Moses, or Isaiah, or Mohammad, or the Buddha or Lao-tzu, or Confucius or Gandhi being asked to give the invocation at a Republican national convention. All the world's major religions started out powered by the left-wing passions of justice, hope, and compassion for the powerless. In their own flawed way they are classics, classics in the art of spotting and targeting exploitation of the have-nots by the haves. Filled as they are with lots of nasty flotsam and jetsam picked up on their voyage through the chaos of history, the world's religions are still at root left-wingers.

Of course, aberrant piety tones down the heroes and heroines of these religions and baptizes them into the cult of the cozy, where the well salaried and well caloried dwell. Look at what they did to Jesus's mother, Mary. Much of the Mary-cult presents her as the queen of the Stepford Wives. In life she was a rebel. The Gospels allowed her one little speech and it was a blockbuster. She began cagily, putting power-holding listeners at ease: "My soul doth magnify the Lord and my spirit rejoices in God my savior." Harmless enough. The power holders could say, "Magnify away there, little lady; you'll do no harm." But a few verses later she tore into the rich and privileged, routing the "arrogant of heart" and the "monarchs" and lifting the humble and the poor on high! She was into the redistribution of wealth and power. Her short speech has been called "one of the most revolutionary documents in all literature, containing three separate revolutions"—moral, political, and economic.[6] No wonder they never let her talk again. She scared the guys!

This compassion, justice hunger, and hope—the passions of healthy left-wingism—found form in the Catholic social justice tradition, which draws on centuries of theories of justice.[7]

Of course, the next question is "Where did all this good

social justice stuff go?" How did it get smothered in the pelvic orthodoxy obsessions of much of contemporary Catholicism?

Good question.

The progressive tradition has been reactivated by Catholic feminists and Latin American liberation theologians, and it is alive and well in Catholic peace groups like Pax Christi and in Catholic lay groups like Call to Action and Voice of the Faithful. It never died out in Dorothy Day and her Catholic Worker movement. But it definitely got shoved out of the Catholic mainstream. Catholic pews have been emptying and its "bare ruined choirs" are bewailed. There is a reason for that. Catholicism suffered a terrible blanding over time as it lost touch with its fiery justice core. In a world with deserts spreading, oceans swelling, and bombs bursting in every air, all sources of moral energy are needed to save this self-destructive species that dares to call itself *sapiens*.

I once attended the inauguration of a newly completed church and educational building in Towson, Maryland. The proud pastor had invited the distinguished Paul Lehmann of New York's Union Theological Seminary to preach. Professor Lehmann mounted the pulpit, looked out into the sea of happy faces in that beamingly well-lit building, and opened with these words: "Do you know what you have built here? A resplendent mausoleum. It stands incandescent in the glow of its own irrelevance as the dynamics of the time rush to pass it by."

After they revived the pastor, Dr. Lehmann went on to

suggest that it might not be so, if Christians could read the signs of the times and find the renewable moral energies of their religion and apply them with smarts and courage to a world in terminal peril.

This book is a wake-up call to the somnambulant religious left.

Good Sex
(Even Catholics Can Have It)

Catholics have been called the leaders in the "Just say no to sex" pack. *No* to stem cell research. *No* to contraception. *No* to abortion. *No* to same-sex marriage. Even *no* to the safest of safe sex, masturbation. Now, if you can't even say yes to masturbation, where no one gets pregnant, no one gets an STD, and someone has a wonderful time, you don't seem to have much to add to the modern conversation about sex . . . or to any other conversation either.

But wait. Don't just blame Catholics.

Secular, "sophisticated" USA is weird city when it comes to sex. Secular society has not exorcized this jumbled message we give our youth: "Sex is dirty; save it for someone you really love." A little cross-cultural comparison can make the point.

At a meeting I attended of scholars from the world's various religions, a Chinese scholar reported that in China now they are starting to put free condoms in hotel drawers. Mustering as straight a face as I could, I said, "We don't do that in the United States. Instead, we put Bibles in motel drawers. We believe that if a couple come to have sex and find the Bible, they will read that instead." With an equally strained straight face, the Chinese scholar asked, "Have you any data?" I replied, "Yes, a very high rate of unplanned pregnancies."

It is easy to imagine the furor that would ensue if free condoms were put in motels and hotels in the United States alongside the mouthwash and hand cream. The same nation that impeaches presidents for having sex but winks at undeclared wars and corporate corruption would erupt in indignation. Our theocratic and Puritan sensibilities would recoil. Politicians would pander righteously and palaver endlessly until those offending condoms were gone. In many ways, the United States is a functioning (or dysfunctioning) theocracy. The First Amendment hides this fact from view.

Let us sing praises to the First Amendment. Its purpose was not to banish religion from life; its purpose was to ensure that public policy will not be made by alleged divine inspiration but by reasoned discourse. In areas of sexuality and reproduction, the First Amendment has failed. Alleged divine inspiration *is* national policy on embryonic stem cell research and therapeutic cloning. And even when national policy and constitutional law permit women to choose abortion, the theocratic culture rebels and manages by harassment, political pressure, and terror to make abortion unavailable in 80 percent of the counties of the nation.

How did we get this way?

The inability to face our sexuality, in Western culture, is to a great extent religiously grounded, with historical Christianity bearing enormous blame. The Jewish forebears of

Christianity were often more sensible about sex and, in the Song of Solomon, could even sing paeans of praise to its many pleasures. Christians choked on all of that and saw sex in the direst of terms, and this dreary view has had a noxious impact on the history of the West. A brief look at that history follows—and then a look at the rediscovery of sexual joy now ongoing in Catholic and other Christian circles.[1]

AUGUSTINE, THE "BROODING NEUROTIC"

Many thinkers come and go, making nary a blip in the movement of history. Augustine, the fifth-century bishop of Hippo in Africa, was not one of them.[2] He had a gifted pen. His Latin was exquisite, and he had a well-cocked eye to his impact on history. He made sure that multiple copies of his writings were made. He succeeded, and some of his worst ideas were the most successful. After enjoying sex for a number of years, he took an antisexual turn and seemed thereafter hell-bent on making sure no one else ever enjoyed it.

Augustine saw sexual passion and sexual pleasure as the conduit for a kind of spiritually stigmatizing "original sin" that was passed on to all our children. So heinous and infectious was the passionate pleasure of parents that led to conception that each little newborn was spiritually blighted and in need of redemptive baptism to cleanse its little soul. (Had Augustine known of cloning he would have loved it. Then the baby could be born clean as a whistle, uncontaminated by any parental sexual pleasure.) Small wonder some speak of "ecclesiogenic psychoneurosis."

Augustine's horror of sexual pleasure actually made him get silly. Augustine misunderstood the biblical creation stories of Genesis as referring to a past paradise that existed, somewhere in the Middle East, until the first humans were expelled for their sins. Actually, those stories are a poetic picturing of what life could be if we rose to our moral and aesthetic potential. It could be a paradise where we and nature live in harmony in a social order knit together with compassion and justice and beauty.

At any rate, Augustine was asked whether in this "paradise lost" there was sexual activity. He allowed that there would have been, to permit reproduction. People then asked if there would have been sexual pleasure in paradise. None, said he. Some practical people raised the question as to how in the world men could get their penises readied for action without sexual pleasure. Augustine's answer: by sheer willpower. After all, he noted, even in our current fallen state some people can move one ear (and the truly gifted, two ears) simply by willing it. Surely men could have elevated their penises in paradise with a hefty act of the will.

In a triumph of common sense, the doubters continued to doubt. Augustine, with his back against the wall, was driven to find new examples of feats of the will. He turned to flatulence, noting that some people could produce it by mere willpower: "Some can produce at will odorless sounds from their breech, a kind of singing from the other end."[3] Alas, all of that to defend his compulsive and sick rejection of sexual pleasure and delight.

Augustine, then, is a major culprit in the Christian attack

on sexual pleasure. He gave us a major theological root for sex as "dirty." And this root dug deep, then sprouted upward and spread like a kudzu vine.

Through most of Christian history, sexual pleasure, even in marriage, was long thought to be sinful. And the rule was: the more pleasure, the more sin. William of Auxerre in the thirteenth century said that a holy man who has sex with his wife and finds it hateful and disgusting commits no sin. He added, with poignant regret (and a bit of insight), that "this, however, seldom happens."

The twelfth-century Petrus Cantor opined that sex with a beautiful women was a greater sin since it caused greater delight. His point was debated, however. His contemporary Alain de Lille demurred, saying sex with a beautiful woman was less sinful because the man was "compelled by the sight of her beauty," and "where the compulsion is greater, the sin is slighter." (Taken to its logical extreme, this would justify the rape of overwhelmingly beautiful women.)

Catholicism decided that only celibate hands can administer the sacraments.[4] The message is clear: sexuality is incompatible with spirituality. Sex is dirty, spirituality sublime. (Recent scandals among the Catholic clergy relate to this taboo. You can't just declare a whole class of people sexless and expect it to work. It would be like trying to elevate your penis with pleasure-free willpower.)

So it came to pass that Catholics and other Christians pumped a lot of bad notions of sex and sexual pleasure into Western culture. Let that be candidly admitted.

Christianity, however, need not shoulder all the blame

for Western sexual neurosis. Science chipped in. The first psychiatry textbook published in the United States said that masturbation "produces seminal weakness, impotence, dysury, tabes dorsalis, pulmonary consumption, dyspepsia, dimness of sight, vertigo, epilepsy, hypochondriasis, loss of memory, manalgia, fatuity and death."[5] Other experts thought this listing terribly incomplete and added that it also caused senility, stupidity, melancholy, homosexuality, suicide, hysteria, mania, religious delusions, auditory hallucination, conceit, defective offspring, and eventually racial decay. The masturbator, it was said, is incapable "of any generous impulse or act of loyalty; he is dead to the call of his family, his country, or of humanity."[6]

How many gentle masturbators reading this would like to plead guilty to those charges?

Errors about sexuality do not remain on the written page. They invade human life and poison it, leading to destructive behavior and sickness. In 1953 Alfred Kinsey and his colleagues, in *Sexual Behavior in the Human Female*, reported that Christianity had had a negative impact on women's sexual pleasure; the more devout they were, the fewer orgasms they had. A more recent study contradicts their findings, saying that "in general, having a religious affiliation was associated with higher rates of orgasm for women."[7] Clearly ethnic cultural variables make it difficult to pinpoint religious influences on anything as specific as orgasm rates. An Irish Catholic is not the same as an Italian Catholic or a Kenyan Catholic. Still, it is beyond dispute that there are religious influences on how comfortable or uncomfortable people are with their sexuality.

In the United States, where religious sexual neurosis took deep root in the dominant culture, the results show up in what I have called "the surprised virgin syndrome," referring to a controlling dishonesty and inability to admit—much less cherish—our capacity for sexual joy. Counselors are familiar with young women, pregnant before they are ready for pregnancy (and pregnancy is a long-term condition and commitment), who claim they do not know "how it happened," as though the onset of sexual ardor were not noticeable. (In response to this, I conducted a subscientific study of one subject, myself, and I can now report this finding: when you are in a relationship that is about to go sexual, you actually do notice it.)

More honest cultures face their sexuality and prepare for it with sexual education and contraceptive availability. Statistics tell the tale. "Each year, one million American teenage girls become pregnant, a per-thousand rate twice that of Canada, England, and Sweden, and ten times that of the Netherlands."[8] The research indicates that there are much higher rates of sexual activity in these other countries, but far fewer pregnancies. Contraceptive availability is key, along with honesty about when a relationship is about to go sexual. Recent studies indicate some welcome improvement in this regard in the United States, showing that U.S. teens are not having less sex, but are finally starting to have safer sex and fewer pregnancies.[9]

Still, studies in the United States show that three-quarters of teens say that their first intercourse was unplanned and a majority of them say they wish they had been older when they had their first intercourse. The broad discomfort with sex discourages communication between teens and parents. This is tragic, since studies show that healthy candor about sex between parents and children helps to postpone the time and the circumstances of first intercourse.

One might think that the puritanical horror of sex has been dissipated in a culture where sex is used ubiquitously in the marketplace to promote sales, and frenzied pornography abounds. However, as theologian Grace Jantzen observes, this obsession reflects the historical Christian obsession and is really "the same preoccupation, turned inside out." The addiction to pornography is fueled by discomfort with sex. It has been suggested that pornography might dull our feeling for the other—in effect, killing love.

So it would seem that religion and sex are not happy bedfellows and that religion has nothing to offer but cruel taboos. Surprise! That is not the case. Christianity and Catholicism, in spite of their long history of demeaning sexuality, have resources to rethink the beauties of sexual pleasure, and some of the healthy moral energies of these traditions are being revived and developed. At the same time, as the interest in "spirituality" is rising, links are being discovered between the sexual and the sacred, and sexual and religious interests are moving in new and fascinating tandem.

SPIRITUALITY: THE NEW RELIGION

Spirituality is more popular than religion. People who would not darken the door of a church, temple, or mosque are open to discussion of spirituality. The left-wing investigative magazine *Mother Jones* devoted a whole issue to spirituality ("Believe It or Not: Spirituality Is the New Religion").[10] Books and articles appear on spirituality in the workplace.[11] In point of fact, morality, spirituality, and religion are concentric circles. Each can be defined as a response to the sacred. "Sacred" is the highest encomium in the human lexicon. It is the superlative of precious. It is where valuation dips into mystery.

Some of our value experiences are literally ineffable; we can't explain them. "Why is this flesh so precious?" I would ask myself as I cradled my ten-year-old son Danny in my arms. His dwarfed body was wasted, as was his mind, by Hunter's syndrome, and he was near death, but I handled him with all the reverence with which I used to handle the sacraments when I was a priest. There are moments when love and reverence intertwine. Indeed, love at its best is charged with reverence.

Jean-Paul Sartre, late in his life, met some former students in a park in Paris. They had their three-month-old baby with them. Sartre took the baby in his arms, and later he wrote that he realized, with a kind of mystical intensity, that if you took all of his life's work—and he was the best-known philosopher of the twentieth century—and balanced it against the smiling preciousness he held in his arms, it all would seem almost weightless by comparison. The words "sacred" and "sanctity of life" attempt to describe such ecstatic moments.

Neither Sartre's nor my experience admits of explanation. And that brings us a step further in knowing what spirituality is. Spirituality is born in the affections—in the deepest part of the affections that the medievals called mystical. It is our appropriate response to values that transcends our paltry powers of analysis. (There can be false spirituality. There are misplaced sacreds that don't merit our reverence: We can worship our selves egotistically. We can worship our nations in the pandemic religion known as nationalism. We can also idolize our gender or our race or our sexual orientation.) True spirituality reacts appropriately and enthusiastically to the value of human life and to the wild beauty of terrestrial life with which we are kith and kin.

MARKS OF A HEALTHY SPIRITUALITY

Drawing upon Jewish, Christian, and even specifically Catholic spiritual resources, let me boldly dare to suggest three signals and signs of a healthy spirituality. From Catholicism, I draw especially on its strong tradition of justice theory and its poetic liturgical powers. Justice theory relates to spirituality and healthy religion. The Catholic Church has always believed the symbol to be mightier than the word and so has something to offer regarding the natural liturgy of sexually expressed love.

The elements, then, of a healthy spirituality are:

1. a release from the isolation of egotism;
2. a passion for the beauty of justice;
3. an undefeatable conviction that hope and joy can be at home in this universe.

Egotism crushes any sense of interdependency and mutuality; it misses the fact that life, all life, is a shared glory, a miracle of energy that merits an explosion of awe, reverence, appreciation, wonder, and a sense of giftednesss. Next, spirituality that does not pulse with a hunger for *justice* for all is specious and a fraud. *Hope* is a recognition that the possibilities of life, with all its bloody blows, outweigh its debits. As for *joy*, the old rabbis had it right when they said, "We will have to give account on the judgment day of every good thing which we refused to enjoy when we might have done so." [12] A true spirituality is convinced that, against all the odds, ecstasy, not misery, is our destiny. Spirituality is baptism by immersion in the stunningness and promise and beauty of life.

ENTER SEX

Good sex is spiritually healthy or it's not good sex. But what is sex? Anyone after puberty has some working definition of *what* sex is. For some, "having sex" is just one of the myriad pleasures available to us. Thus a couple might take a walk together, share a beer or a game of tennis, or they might just have sex . . . putting all these activities on a par. In this simplistic and reductionistic view, as long as the participants consent, there is no other consideration.

Conservative theologians, on the contrary, define "having sex" as the "marital act," meaning that sexual activity is moral language that says that the participants are heterosexual and married. Any other form of sex—premarital, masturbatory, or homosexual—is wrong. This arbitrarily and arrogantly limits the possible moral meanings and advantages of sexual activity. It ignores such views as those of Catholic philosophers Daniel Dombrowski and Robert Deltete of the Jesuit Seattle University: "A rich spiritual life is not necessarily hindered by, and may actually be enhanced by, premarital sexual relations," if those relationships "exhibit mutual consent and mutual agapic respect." (Agapic is from the Greek *agape*; in biblical literature, it is the full flowering of healthy love.) They add, "To loosen the connection between moral sexual relations and marriage does not imply abandonment of a sacramental view of marriage wherein the *best* sex is that which enriches a lifelong agapic commitment between two individuals." That is the "best" but not the only good way of expressing love sexually. They add that the same can be said for good homosexual relationships.[13] Obviously this is new language from Catholic sources, part of the ongoing Catholic Enlightenment being led by the laity and lay scholars.

SEX AS LITURGY

For humans, sex (as with everything else for humans) is more than it appears to be. At a purely physical level, it releases unconscious springs of playfulness and relaxes tensions and frictions born of the struggling, deliberative part of our lives. Sex is fun. But sex is serious fun. It is fun with an agenda. In fertile heterosexuals it can make babies. Its biological intimacy makes it a conduit for disease. And sex is serious because it is packed with psychological and liturgical power. In frivolous encounters, this force may not ignite, but it is ever there, "winking at the brim."

I define sex as a natural liturgy. A liturgy consists of symbols, and we use symbols all the time. From handshakes to bows and waves, to nose rubbing, kisses, hugs, and smiles, we speak not just in words, but also in symbols. The word "symbol" comes from the Greek *syn*, meaning with or together, and *ballein*, to throw. A symbol throws together more meaning than we can say in mere words . . . unless those words are poetized, and thus symbolized. A liturgy is a coordinated group of symbols. Some liturgies are conventional and contrived. They are "made up" and they vary from culture to culture. Irish weddings and Nigerian weddings are different.

Natural liturgies do not vary. They are inborn. Some of the externals will vary, but in substance, they are intrinsic to our humanity. For humans, a meal is a natural liturgy. There are two aspects to a proper meal: one is physical (food is essential) and the other is symbolic. The symbolic aspect, somewhat surprisingly, is more important than the food. You don't invite people to a meal because they are hungry or low on proteins. You invite them to show love and respect and to celebrate, and this brings you directly into symbols. Crystal, silverware, precious china, candles, music, lighting. It's as though you are setting up an altar. (It is not surprising that many religions use a meal as their central liturgy. It is already a liturgy; they simply add religious motifs.)

Even the food in the meal liturgy is wrapped in symbolism. The food is not served unceremoniously in a vat, or given intravenously. It is garnished in lovely symbols and presented with elegance. The main business of this dining liturgy is communication of love and respect. These expressions are necessary even for digestion. If you had to dine with someone you despised, your digestion would rebel.

Now to the natural liturgy called sex. Like a meal, sex involves both physical realities and powerful symbolism. Though one encounter or another may not show it, sex is powerful. Sexually charged love is especially bonding, and, when frustrated, leads to the breaking of hearts or worse. Sex really does "make love" and you do get "involved." There is bonding power in the sexual meeting.

Interestingly, the physical facts of sex aptly symbolize what sex tends to do psychologically. There is not just physical nakedness; there is emotional nakedness. We trust our partner with full exposure of our passions and needs. We shed our emotional clothes and cosmetics and present ourselves as we are. Sex is a huge act of trust, a hopeful abandonment of our normal defenses. It takes many delightful forms and may involve various kinds of penetration and envelopment; this symbolizes the emotional interweaving that occurs in sexually charged friendship. The lover may remain only an experience, but more often she or he tends to become a way of life. Sex bonds, and bonds powerfully. The immature may not be ready to deal with its force.

THE WEDDING OF SEXUALITY
AND SPIRITUALITY

The touchstones of healthy spirituality, *respect, justice, hope,* and *joy*, are the hallmarks of good sex. Sex with a partner you do not respect is corrosive. It used to be said *animal humanum post coitum triste*, or "humans after love-making are sad." And according to the poet Yeats, "a pity beyond all telling is hid in the heart of love." That can happen. Sex awakens hopes for intimacy and the priceless gift of mutual trust. The sadness of prostitution is that it brings together hopeless partners; it fails to blend sex with our moral hopes. That is sad. Sex workers are victims, and Jesus was remarkably kind to them.

Sex wrapped in mutual caring is exalting; it blends body and spirit in orgasmic unity. It affirms our beauty as persons.

Pleasure is what sex is about, yet stoic philosophy invaded Western culture with the idea that sexual pleasure is presumed guilty until proven innocent. Only procreative intent could bring acquittal. Such nonsense! Sex rarely has anything to do with procreation. The old axiom "Listen to your body" was misapplied here. We listened too much to the penis when we should have sought an audience with the clitoris. Sexual ethics has been caught in a penis monologue. The penis has divided loyalties and multiple missions; it is concerned with procreation and waste removal. The clitoris is single-minded. Its one goal, as ethicist Susan Ross says, is "exquisite female sexual pleasure." Clitoral wisdom is our need.

The penis has for too long dominated the sexual imagination of the Western world. Dismissing all the pleasuring possibilities available via "outercourse," the great sexual heresy is that "no intercourse = no sex." Without penile penetration of the vagina, sex has not happened. Bill Clinton was a preacher and practitioner of this aberrant gospel.

The hatred of women's sexual pleasure, going all the way to enforced clitoridectomy, actually evinces a perverted sense of its importance. No wonder weak men fear it. It contains a liberative message. Part of homophobia comes from the fact that gay and lesbian sex does not seek validation in reproductivity and is simply and honestly about relationship, love, and pleasure. That is threatening to those who are pleasure-phobic.

THE SEXUAL REVIVAL

Religions are mutants. They have to be. They're covered by the "change or die" rule. And when they change, history turns a corner, because these behemoths that we call "religions" are the underwriters of much that we call culture, and culture is the womb that shapes us. For good or for ill, religion is a big-time player in the power drama of life. Ignore it at your peril.

Even big old hoary religions change. Like Catholicism, for example. The Vatican is sternly rebuking the incoming tide, but the waters of change are washing over it.

A story is worth a thousand pictures. Here's one:

A few years ago, in Maputo, Mozambique, the Catholic bishop came to say Mass in one of his parishes. Afterward he took questions from the congregation. The first question went straight to the pelvic zone, where too many Catholic energies have been concentrated: "What is the Church's position on condom use?" The question, posed from an AIDS-ravaged continent, related to the Vatican's weird and lethal teaching that condoms cannot be used even if one's partner is HIV positive.

"God clearly tells us that we must protect life at all costs. Not to do so is a serious sin against God," the bishop replied, in what sounded like the beginning of a hellfire and damnation blast. But then the bishop continued: "What does this mean to you and to me? It means that A is for abstinence and looking around at all of you today, many of you cannot live by this advice. Let us be realistic; few if any of you can abstain. Which brings us to B, be faithful. Some of you are faithful . . . many of you are not. So that leaves us with C, condoms. Now many of you believe that condoms are a crime against God, that wasted semen is a sin, but I am here today to tell you otherwise. You see, if you are HIV positive and you have unprotected sex and infect someone, you have, in the eyes of God, committed murder. Or if you are HIV negative and you have unprotected sex with someone who is infected, you have, in the eyes of God, committed suicide." He concluded: "So, my children, wearing a condom is not a sin . . . not wearing one is."

The congregation took this advice and ran with it. According to a witness of this liturgy, "Sunday church services will never be the same, as now, every Sunday, part of the celebration is the blessing of the condoms. That's right, the BLESSING OF THE CONDOMS." [14]

The South African Catholic bishop Kevin Dowling gives the same message and no thunderbolts from the Vatican have struck him. In 2005, 47 percent of pregnant women in his diocese tested positive for HIV. "The only solution we have at the moment is condoms," says Bishop Dowling. [15] Persistent rumors, always denied but always recurrent, say that the Vatican itself is planning a switch on the issue of condoms. Reality is bypassing dogma; a quiet revolution is under way. Polls of Catholics on the pelvic issues are coming into line with other moderns. The grip of the hierarchy is loosening and the civic effects of this will not be slight in any country where Catholicism is a fact of life.

WOMEN THEOLOGIANS
TO THE RESCUE

Sexual pleasure, rather than being suspect, is bounteously filled with good human news. Christian ethicist Mary Pellauer, in her essay "The Moral Significance of Female Orgasm," in the *Journal of Feminist Studies in Religion* (1993), says that "flesh has the capacity to burst me open to existence" so that our "connections to the rest of the universe are felt . . . as pleasurable." Patricia Beattie Jung says, "Our sexuality draws us into one another's arms—and consequently into an awareness of and concern about the needs of that other." Audre Lorde, in her essay "Uses of the Erotic," says that the experience of sexual pleasure can stir up in women a sense of their self-worth. Once women taste such delights, they can begin to demand "what is in accord with joy in other areas" of their lives. Women will "begin to give up . . . being satisfied with suffering, and self-negation, and with the numbness" that the macho culture demands of them. Mary Pellauer agrees, saying that "to touch and be touched in ways that produce sweet delight affirms, magnifies, intensifies and redoubles the deep value of our existence." Sa'diyya Shaik writes that in Islam it is recognized that "sexual union has the possibilities for unparalleled mystical unveilings and experiences of the Divine." To call sex "dirty" is a calumny.[16]

Notice that this talk of sex covers all the bases of a healthy spirituality. Respect for self and others, joyful affirmation of our hopes for justice and for life. It's all there. That's good sex, and that's good spirituality.

Our sense of what is normal sex is socially constructed, and much of that social construction is poisonous, sitting on our sexuality like a noxious miasma. Healthier winds are blowing this damnable gas out to sea and we are beginning to see that in moments of truthful sexual joy a sacred beauty is born.

Male and Female Were We Made (With Some Variations on Those Themes)

Imagine this scenario: You are walking down a dark street late at night. Suddenly you become aware of two young people quickly moving up on you from behind. Startled, you turn, then breathe a quick sigh of relief, saying: "Oh, thank God it's two guys; I was terrified it might be two girls."

Or imagine this: You hear of the horrific bombing of the federal building in Oklahoma City, killing hundreds of people including children. Your first thought is: "I hope they catch the women who did that!"

Or you hear that there is a rape every six or seven minutes in the United States and you ask, "Are the rapists usually men or women?"

Stereotyping is false generalization, but not all generalizations are false. Boys and girls are different by nature and by nurture.

One of the faults of contemporary journalism is the "on the one hand, on the other hand" egalitarianism that must make both sides in every dispute look equal. "Otherwise it's just not right! Why it's even un-American!" Meanwhile, back in the real world, right and wrong are never so evenly packaged, especially in issues of gender justice. Refreshed with that caution, let's tackle sexism and then its soul mate, heterosexism.

Here is another story that is also worth a thousand pictures. In 1972, the results of some tests were reported in *Science* magazine. Fictitious descriptions of prospective academic candidates were sent for evaluation to a group of male departmental chairs. The paragraphs describing the candidates were identical. All that the investigator did was occasionally change the name and sex of the candidate. When that happened—when female replaced male—the ranking plunged. The male candidates were thought worthy of higher ranks and more worthy of tenure, even though the credentials presented were identical.[1]

Now I think we can safely assume that when these chairmen pulled into their home driveways that day, their wives or daughters would not look out the window and say: "Here comes that male chauvinist pig!" No, they most likely would have said: "Dad's home!" The investigators, however, could have rushed in right after Dad and said to his wife and daughters: "This man really is a male chauvinist. The very sight of your gender on a page so filled him with thoughts of inferiority that he made a fool of himself, and we nailed the rascal."

Sexism is the stubbornly ingrained belief that women are inferior. We're not born with it. In fact, with our first impressions as sucklings, it's the last thing we could believe. But things change and prejudice is born, and nothing fuels prejudice like advantage. If a prejudice and its attendant myths give you unearned privileges, prejudice becomes an addictive drug.

Looking at American society, we see that for two hundred years we have had preferential affirmative action for white males, giving them 90 to 100 percent of all the top jobs in church, state, business, and academe. That is a sweet arrangement for white males. And it would be a splendid arrangement for all if 90 to 100 percent of the talent in the human race were white and male. Since it's not, it's a self-inflicted wound.

RELIGIONS AND MALE DOMINATION

All the major religions are troves containing both gems and junk. It is the gems we are after, but the junk must also be checked out since it is often more influential than the gems. Catholicism has much on the junk side when it comes to male hubris, and that should be faced more squarely than is usually the case. Then we can see if the Catholic story has any antidotal gems for the problems it has helped to create.

When I was a student in Europe in 1955, I attended Mass in the little German village of Dachau, a few miles away from the eponymous concentration camp. At the time I gave little thought to the lurid irony of that lovely little church.

Thanks to a concordat with Nazi Germany, such churches were kept open under Nazi rule. Hitler, indeed, wanted to be sure that all churches were staffed with priests, but his interests were not pious. The deal he struck with the Catholic Church kept the lid on possible resistance from that powerful corner of the Reich. So what was in the deal for Pope Pius XII?

Catholic theologian John Pawlikowski puts it this way: "The theology of Pius XII was one that largely defined the Church in its essence as the institution through which the vital ingredients for human salvation—Mass and the sacraments—are made available to the human community. Since the continued existence of the Church was of the very highest priority, the goal had to be to keep the Church alive no matter what the cost in non-Catholic lives."[2] To keep the sacramental system of the Church going, the Jews and the millions of other victims had to be viewed, in professor Nora Levin's terms, as "unfortunate expendables."[3] This is a horror. During the war, Catholic services continued and the smoke of incense wafted out church windows and rose to mingle in the air with the smoke of the murdered dead.

Now, with seminaries closing and parts of the Catholic world not seeing a priest from one end of a year to the next, the sacramental system is shutting down. Those priestless areas do have trained catechists, married men and women, who could be ordained priests tomorrow. The sacramental system would then be restarted. But no. While critique of the Holocaust could be muted to save the sacraments, the exclusion of women (and men contaminated by marriage to them) cannot be eased in the same cause. Indentured hatred of women, sexism in full noxious bloom, is the only explanation of that.

The sexist myth was deeply rooted in culture and in religion. Woman's potential was shrunken. She was a brood mare. "She will be saved through motherhood," says the Christian Epistle to Timothy (1 Tim. 2:15). Without it she is, in that belatedly obsolescent word, a "spinster." In ancient Israel, "since everything centered on the man, polygamy was the natural type of marriage for Israelites, for several wives do more than one to satisfy the demand for children. If a wife gave her husband insufficient children, he might take secondary wives and concubines, and be encouraged by his wife to so do."[4]

Augustine pondered all this and concluded: "I do not see what other help woman would be to man if the purpose of generating was eliminated."[5] Add to this that God in Israel was imaged mainly as a man, with Goddess images vigorously suppressed, and in orthodox Christianity a human male was divinized, saying that when God had a choice the choice was to be a man. This is not the kind of acidic soil from which verdant gender justice could grow.

Religions can be putrid pools as well as healthy streams fed with spring water. In Christian scripture, wives are told to "be subject to your husbands as to the Lord." What a message! Be subject to your men as if they were God and do so "in everything" (Eph. 5:22–24). Religious patriarchy in full force.

But then, in a breakthrough text that became a mantra in the early Jesus movement, the message was that all the hostile divisions between Jews and Greeks, slaves and free people, men and women are all dissolved, "for you are all one person in Christ Jesus" (Gal. 3:28). This meant that in the vision of this rabbi called Jesus, alienation and outgrouping within the human family were proscribed. This is a remarkably early expression of feminist and egalitarian thinking. Small wonder that women thronged to the early Jesus movement.[6] Patriarchy soon refastened its grip, but the liberative message had been unleashed and would bob to the surface at various times in history.

The faithful in text-based religions are rarely faithful to the best (that's sad) or the worst (thank heavens) in their traditions. Sam Harris, in his popular book *The End of Faith*, produces a scathing caricature of contemporary Islam by piling horror text after horror text from the Qur'an and Islamic literature.[7] He gets so carried away with his rhetoric that he reaches the frantic conclusion that if these Qur'anic people got nuclear weapons, we'd best launch "a nuclear first strike of our own," even if that means the death of "tens of millions of innocent civilians."[8]

Down, boy!

Civilizations do not unfold through a faithful following of foundational script. Texts do not a people make, whether in religion or in politics. Read the brilliant writings of early American thinkers and then think of George W. Bush and the people who made him president twice. You can no more judge contemporary Islam on the basis of Islamic texts than you can judge your local rabbi and his congregation on the savage texts of Leviticus. Texts are important and meant to be studied, but not simplistically as nontheologian Harris does. He would have been well advised to finish his course work in neuroscience and then take some university courses in the complexity of the religious phenomenon and its literature.

All religions carry a lot of sickness in their train. And yet they have also been the vehicles for some of the most civilizing insights in human history. When the brilliant and morally creative early Hebrews decided that monarchs could no longer claim the title "Image of God" for themselves, they blazed the first steps of the trail that led to modern democratic theory. When symbols are seized and given new meaning, history does a U turn. The Hebrews were saying that if you want to see "the image of God," you don't need to go to the pharaoh's or king's palace. Just look at your children, or your grandmother sitting by the fire, or go to the reflecting pond and look in. You are looking at the image of God as these people saw it. That insight eventually pulled the rug out from under the "divine right of kings" nonsense. We're all in debt to it.

DO CATHOLICS HAVE ANYTHING TO OFFER?

Yes.

For one thing, women.

For the first time in Catholic history, women have entered into intellectual life en masse. They were there before but were totally outnumbered. Fifty years ago, "Catholic theologian" meant a priest. No more. And as women entered theology they quickly embraced feminism—so quickly it caused wonder. No need to wonder. In Catholicism the divine did not manage to stay masculine. Mary, Jesus's mother, is the reason why.

This illustrates again the gap between text and reality in social movements like religions. The keepers of orthodoxy insisted on very precise differences in the reverence for Mary and the worship due her son. That orthodoxy did not translate into broad Catholic practice or piety. Whether it is Our Lady of Lourdes or Our Lady of Guadalupe or any of the other images of Mary, she is not a subordinate figure in Catholic piety. From Latin America to Ireland, the statues of Mary overwhelmingly predominate; Jesus is an also-ran. In Holy Rosary Church in Milwaukee there is a prominent statue of Mary at the altar. She is holding the baby Jesus in her arms. St. Dominic is kneeling in front of her and she is giving him the rosary beads. The two males in this cast are Jesus, a helpless baby, and Dominic, on his knees receiving the holy gift from the strong woman who is clearly in charge of both. Small wonder that in imagined apparitions in the Catholic world, Mary, not Jesus, always has the featured role. Orthodoxy be damned: Catholics for centuries knelt before and prayed to Mary. Their primary God was a woman.

The number of Catholic women saints who were as such also tinged with divinity gave further relief from the masculinization of the deity that the Jewish and Christian sacred texts tried to establish. Catholic women were ripe for the feminization of God—and ripe for shaking off the coils of outrageous sexism.

Groups like Catholics for a Free Choice formed to champion the right of women, not governments, to make decisions on abortion. The group called Dignity defends lesbian, gay, bisexual, and transgender rights for Catholics. Voice of the Faithful mobilized Catholic laity with enough power to force the cardinal of Boston, Bernard Law, to resign and flee to Rome for his malfeasance and misfeasance in handling cases of clergy abuse of children. Catholic theology, energized by the infusion of lay blood, stirred from its slumbers and started making distinctions between Vatican theology and Catholic theology, the latter being more broadly based and better informed.

THE RETURN OF JUSTICE

Ancient Israel and early Christianity were cool to love and hot for justice. As one scripture scholar puts it, Jesus was "sparing in his use of the word 'love' [noun or verb]."[9] This was a recognition that justice is the difference between civilization and chaos. Love is great on a one-to-one level, but you can't walk into the State Department and ask, "Have you tried love?" You *can* walk in and demand justice. Justice is the moral currency that holds the country together. Governments are legitimate, and meriting obedience, only insofar as they embody justice.

While not eschewing interpersonal morality, the main thrust of biblical religion was social, economic, and political reform. If human society is clay, said Abraham Heschel, justice is "the mold in which God wants history to be shaped."[10]

Lately, Catholics have revisited their neglected treasures. This biblically grounded justice theory is oxygen in the fight against sexism.

DOING WELL BY DOING GOOD

The Bible writers, on their good days—and they had some awful ones—were practical folk, bottom-line thinkers. Why do justice? Because it pays, and—pay attention!—injustice wrecks you. They dumped the conventional wisdom of the ancients: "Let justice be done should the world perish" (*Fiat justitia, pereat mundus*); instead, they said, "Let justice be done or the world will perish" (*Fiat justitia ne pereat mundus*).

Apply this to sexism and to systems built on the assumption of male superiority, since we live in a man-made (male-made) world. How's it going?

Answer: Have you read any headlines lately?

Second, more direct answer: Poorly!

Inquiring minds can put a little justice analysis to work on that. The leitmotif of Catholic justice theory is the *common good*. The common good is the matrix in which all private good is set. If we didn't have some of it, we would be hiding in our cellars and starving. Looking at sexism from the purview of the common good, the question really is, What impact does it have on *all* of us?

PUTTING THE HUMAN MALE ON THE STAND

Stereotyping that blurs individual differences is not our goal here. There are good men and horrible women. We all know lots of both. My argument here is that macho-masculine culture (and you can toss in some hormonal factors) has in varying ways impeded male sensitivities, giving men (and women influenced by them) distinct debits in moral and religious knowing. At the same time, the experience of women (add "nature" factors if you like) has given them certain advantages in their moral perceptivity. My conclusion will not point to the triumph of femininity over masculinity, but to a hope for a humanity which banishes stunted femininity and macho-masculinity and blends the masculine and the feminine into ever more genuine modalities of the species human.

Now on to the principal liabilities of the macho-masculine blight:

1. Propensity to violence

War is a male preserve, a guy thing. The Amazons, after all, are creatures of myth. Understandably, the military fought the idea of women in arms. Warriors, fortunately, do not always find wars, but the violence infection goes to the roots. Listen to the language of our male-dominated culture: show me your metaphors and I will tell you what you are. The macho-masculine approach to life tends to be aggressive, not caring, engendering, or relational. In such a mind-set, problems are *assaulted*, not solved; diseases are *defeated*, not cured. We wage *war* on illness and social problems. A *killing* is made in the stock market. The Christian cross becomes a *triumph*, and God a *mighty fortress*. The system is to be *beaten*, and the frontiers of knowledge *pushed back*. Even poetry is called a *raid* on the inarticulate. Business language smacks of the terrors of the hunt: you must *corner* the market, *wipe out* the competition, and see that the bull displaces the bear. The male-ruled marketplace is not a gentle zone.

The George W. Bush administration often teaches not only by tragedy but by unwitting comedy. Germany's newsmagazine *Der Spiegel* created a satirical cover for its story of the Bush crusade against evil, in which the president was pictured as a muscle-bound Rambo with an automatic weapon, Dick Cheney became the Terminator, while Condoleezza Rice was Xena, Warrior Princess. Colin Powell was Batman and Donald Rumsfeld was Conan the Barbarian, holding a sword dripping with blood. Not surprisingly, the U.S. ambassador to Germany visited *Der Spiegel*'s editorial office. Surprisingly, he did not come to protest but to order thirty-three poster-size renditions of the cover. Each of Bush's staff pictured on the cover wanted copies.[11]

2. The hierarchical instinct

The second macho-masculine debit flows from the first. The violent seek dominance, not cooperation. In the macho model in state, church, corporation, and family, the motif is hierarchy and control, not communion, harmony, and mutuality. Corporate structures are models of "un-democracy."

One of the Gospel sayings that scholars think may actually be traceable to the historical Jesus criticizes leaders who "lord it over their subjects" and make their subjects "feel the weight of authority." Doing radical surgery on this management style, Jesus said, "That is not to be the way with you . . . whoever wants to be first must be the willing slave of all" (Mark 10:42–45). This stunning challenge didn't survive the macho takeover of the church that eventually followed Jesus's death. A male-run control system moved in, eventually leading to such creations as the papacy. As one theologian put it, Jesus no more planned the current papacy than Sitting Bull planned the Bureau of Indian Affairs. That the papacy has become one of the last remaining forms of absolute monarchy is a sad betrayal of the Jesus revolution in authority. Guys love hierarchy.

3. Pernicious abstractionism

The flight to abstraction is an escape hatch for the violent; it spares them contact with their victims. "Collateral damage" sounds better than murdered babies. Helium-filled abstractions like "national security," "national interest," and "nuclear superiority" can mesmerize the male mind to the undoing of all concrete "security," "interest," and "superiority." "Freedom" and "democracy" are useful abstractions when you are involved in mayhem. The colonel who stood in the ashes of the village of Ben Tre in Vietnam and explained to the press that "we had to destroy this village in order to save it" spoke like a man. Most women would choke on the connection between incinerating and "saving." Condoleezza Rice spoke like a man (thus giving us a warning against stereotyping) in 2006 when she described the bombing and shelling of Lebanon into Stone-Age wreckage as "the birth pangs of a new Middle East." Bombing? Birthing? Really?

4. A bias for consequentialist, bottom-line thinking

In ethics, "consequentialism" is fixated on results—i.e., that is good which has good effects. The pot of gold on the bottom line is all-important. How you got to the bottom line is of diminished interest. Symbolically, consequentialists are engineers (not to disparage all engineers; some of my best friends are engineers, and I really wouldn't mind if my sister married one). But Professor John Dixon makes a suggestive point in his article "The Erotics of Knowing": "Engineering may be the model for the masculine as biology is the model for the feminine."[12] An obsession with results can blind you to the mess you are making on your way to the promised land. Recent U.S. male-dominated foreign policy is illustrative. We are still wrecking countries in order to save them.

5. Hatred of women

Too strong a charge? No. It's a perfect description of macho attitudes toward women. There are only two possible explanations of why in the United States white men dominate.

First possibility: cream has (as cream will) risen to the top. Run a fair, meritocratic race and white guys are sure to win.

But there is a second possibility: put a monopoly in place, keeping all the top spots for guys, and fight every effort to change it. Fight affirmative action. Fight the Equal Rights Amendment but save the monopoly, with all the advantages thereof. That's hostile, and "hatred" is the honest word for it. What is hatred? Hatred is anger with tenure. And the heat stirred by efforts for gender justice signals deep-rooted anger.

SO ARE WOMEN PERFECT?

No. As an example, a lot of women accept, even embrace, victimization and vote for it. That's not perfect. And aggression (passive and active) is one monopoly men have not been able to pull off. That said, women have some advantages by way of nature and nurture that have been sorely missed in the power circles from which women were banished. Let me dare to mention a few:

1. Contentment with bodily existence

At birth, society looks at our crotches and then appoints us to one of two available cultures: the feminine pink or the masculine blue. The feminine culture is filled with the memories and symbols of earthly service of the body and its environment. Men can inseminate and ride off dreamfully into the sunset, but for women, a biological drama of symbiosis that begins with pregnancy and nursing ties them to the moment for months. Indeed, looked at realistically, pregnancy is at least a twenty-five-year condition since our chicks do not fly off quickly into independence.

History as well as biology have seen to it that women are more attuned to values in the concrete. This does not mean that women are less intellectual, but that their intellectuality is more wholesomely rooted in the flesh and earth, where values are rooted. Women have menstrual reminders that life is not lived from the neck up. Male-imposed standards of pulchritude have pressed women to bodily attentiveness.

Jean-Paul Sartre said that the greatest evil of which we are capable is treating as abstract that which is concrete. Women are less apt to do so. The embodied mind is well rooted and less dangerous.

2. Integration of mind and affect

Affectivity is the animating mold of moral "knowing." Moral knowledge is a *feeling* knowledge, based on the affective experience of the worth of people and this generous host of an earth. Those in whom affectivity is less suppressed are more integrated and more reliable in moral judgment. Since civilization rests on moral judgment, this is no small item. Women are less blunted in their affective responses than men. Under the dogma of "Big boys don't cry," little boys have their tear ducts culturally excised and that makes big boys dangerous. Tears are like a pulse. In a world full of sadness, they're a sign of life. They are unfortunately consigned by macho culture to women, leaving men, at least in this respect, a bit dead.

Studies in psychology have shown that the moral judgments of women differ from those of men in that they are more closely tied to "feelings of empathy and compassion and are concerned more with the resolution of 'real-life' as opposed to hypothetical dilemmas."[13] Lawrence Kohlberg's all-male (!) sampling decided women's moral maturity was retarded by contextual and affective "constraints."[14] Wow! Those who are truly not held back by contextual or affective "constraints" are usually constrained in jails. They lack affective bonds to reality. Men who have created the end of the world and stored it in their nuclear silos all in the name of "security" need better affective ties to reality. Women can help.

3. Association with children

Children need to be parented; adults need to be "childed." In the veins of our children, the best rhythms of our humanity flow—trust, celebration, love, hope—and if those gentle rhythms do not prevail, our future is in terminal peril. Children arrive believing in the normative normalcy of joy—i.e., joy is what ought to be. When kids don't find it, they scream. By adulthood many decide that misery is normal and joy an exception (and when you find a bit of it, grab it). That's a cold, right-wing thought, because if misery is normal and many are miserable, so what? It's normal.

Kids don't buy it, and women by nature and by custom are generally better "childed" than men.

I learned this from my retarded son, Danny, who died at age ten of Hunter's syndrome. I remember when first I took him to a doctor. Danny, who knew that joy was normal, rejoiced in the doctor's waiting room. It was full of toys and kids waiting to share their joys and germs with him. Then we went into the doctor's office. Danny continued rejoicing, giving the doctor the benefit of the doubt that he, too, was into joy. Within minutes, Danny had a needle penetrating his precious little bottom. Appropriately, he screamed.

At that moment the cynical adult world would say to Danny: "Live with it, guy. That's where you get it in this life." But Danny would have none of it. This little boy with blighted mind but exquisite affections knew that ecstasy is our destiny and when you don't find it, scream and fight like hell. A lot of nonretarded people don't know that, especially macho men who replace sensitivity with steely grit.

4. Alienation

If you draw a circle and cut me out of it, I will become acutely aware of what is going on inside that circle. In a perverse way, alienation lends light. The alienated must be defensive, and the defensive have big eyes. History has given women this dear-bought advantage. We need what they know.

Sidelining women has hurt us. This doesn't mean that women are completely in the clear. Some, even under the flag of feminism, have matched men in separatism and class-based and race-based hubris. And all men have not ravaged the earth. Some men have been tireless healers and consolers, embodying the best of both the masculine and the feminine. Still, there are gender-based tendencies and trends that play out powerfully in the human drama. It is a service to justice and to the common good to take note of that.

SEXISM AND HETEROSEXISM

In 1811 in Edinburgh, Scotland, Miss Jane Cumming said she spotted two schoolteachers, Miss Marianne Woods and Miss Jane Pirie, having sex. Two persons having sex is something one would notice. The ladies denied it and the case went to court. The case worked its way slowly all the way to the House of Lords, which ruled in 1819 that the ladies seen having sex did not have sex. Their reasoning, if not an epic of wisdom, is surely an epic of something. First, the accuser was a native of India, and the lords ruled that such lascivious behavior might go on in her native India but a British woman would not be capable of it.

Then the lords went deeper, so to speak, into the case. Lawyers argued that the two women could not have had sex because they lacked an instrument of penetration.[15]

As Bernadette Brooten observes, "Across centuries, men share a fundamental assumption about female sexuality, namely that female pleasure requires a penis."[16] That, of course, is pure sexual and sexist imperialism—penisism, if you will—the result of sexual ethics being a penis monologue. The bias against women also struck at their sexuality.

It is a fact of life that prejudice and bias metastasize. The hatred of women is refracted onto men who love men, thereby reducing them to the level of women. Male homosexuals are scorned as "girlie boys," and their sexual pleasure is demeaned and demonized.

It is part of the mind-shrinking quality of prejudice that it misses much of reality. The result is what smart people call "heteronormativity"—i.e., only heterosexual attraction and pleasure is "normal." In the current political mantra, "Marriage is between a man and a woman."

Saying "male and female were we made" is simplistic, since human sexuality does not divide neatly into a dyad. Biology is exuberant and infinitely varied in its sexual preferences and expressions. In *Biological Exuberance: Animal Homosexuality and Natural Diversity*, biologist Bruce Bagemihl shows that heterosexual and homosexual variety is part of our evolutionary heritage as primates. He reports that more than 450 species regularly engage in a wide range of same-sex activities, from copulation to long-term bonding. Even the assumed male/female dimorphism is not fixed in nature. "Many animals live without two distinct genders, or with multiple genders," he says. Finding evidence that our currently preferred social arrangements are exemplified in edifying animal conduct is also doomed. The lovely mallards sometimes form "trio-bonds," with one male and two females or one female with two males.[17] "Doing what comes naturally" really does leave you with a lot of options. If you believe that God is the author and creator of nature, then sexual diversity is a Godly idea. Gay is not just good; it's holy!

Harmful options can be called immoral, but not all the sexual options are self-evidently harmful.

The Catholic hierarchs, lagging again behind the wisdom of the Church, are very upset by same-sex unions. "Disordered," they call them. Help, however, is available to these bishops, right in their own tradition. Same-sex unions are found in the first thousand years of Christianity and were even liturgically celebrated. Rather than fulminating against same-sex unions, the bishops should kneel and say a prayer to Saints Serge and Bacchus, a same-sex couple whose marriage is preserved in a seventh-century icon showing Jesus as the *pronubus* (official witness, "best man") at their wedding.[18]

In its sensible moments, Catholic teaching, relying on the Bible, recognized that people are not prone to celibacy. Indeed, they saw it as a heroic effort when monks and nuns undertook to be celibate throughout their lives. Jesus said of celibacy, "Let those accept it who can" (Matt. 19:12). Very sensible. Voluntary celibacy for a good cause is something some can do, but it was seen as a special talent, a special gift that not all have. The Vatican Council called it "a precious gift of divine grace which the Father gives to some persons," but not to all. Abstaining from all sexual activity is seen by the council as something "unique."[19] You cannot demand from all homosexual people that which is "unique." St. Paul recognizes the same thing when he says, "It is better to marry than to burn" (1 Cor. 7:9). What kind of Gospel "good news" would it be to tell all gay persons that their only choice is to "burn, baby, burn"?

The view that homosexual people are condemned to in-

voluntary celibacy for life is as cruel as it is absurd. And it is
very Catholic to say so. Saints Serge and Bacchus would
agree.

Humanity needs its exuberant diversity, but humans
tend to flee from it. William Sloane Coffin writes, "Diversity
may be the hardest thing for a society to live with—and perhaps the most dangerous thing to live without."[20] The self-
protective hunger for a cowering monism could indeed be
the fatal flaw of our species. We either learn to live with and
exult in the wealth and beauty of our natural and cultural
differences—gender, religious, ethnic, racial, sexual—or we
wither.

3

The Perennial Orphans of American Conscience

Clarence Thomas was head of the Equal Employment Opportunity Commission when I lunched with him at Drake University Law School. I had just given a talk on affirmative action, which he attended. I had not been gentle to the Reagan administration on issues of race and had remarked that it surely had not been a triumph of nobility when the administration removed a vegetable from school lunches by declaring ketchup to be vegetable enough. Afterward, I was led to my table for lunch, and who to my wondering eyes should appear but Clarence Thomas and his two assistants. They were to be my table companions.

The mood was grim. Clarence grumbled, for openers, that he had no time for all this "Republican bashing." One of his two African American assistants jumped in, saying that "that ketchup decision was very complicated." I replied, "So complicated that it could not be handled with a phone call saying, 'Give the poor kids back their vegetable'?" Some mumbling about liberal naivete followed. It was then that Clarence declared stoutheartedly that he was opposed to people who feel that the government has to do it all for you. "You have to do it for yourself," he asserted.

Were I a diary writer, I would not have listed it among my "lunches most pleasant." It did not enhance digestion. I boarded my plane after lunch quietly burping and thinking, "I wonder what plans they have for that man!" Time would tell.

Here was an African American beneficiary of preferential affirmative action (with more preference still to come) denouncing the program and identifying with the oppressors who would kill this belated and long-due remedy. Self-hatred could not be made of more pathetic stuff.

T he American triumph," James Baldwin said, "was to make black people despise themselves."[1] Oppression is never successful until the victims begin to hate themselves, and American racism has been a searing success. The energy that drives this triumph is the enduring belief in the inferiority of African Americans and the superiority of whites; that is the heart and soul of racism. Derrick Bell, a professor of law and an African American, goes to the quick of it: "The burden of racism has scarred us all, and there are few whites who at some level of their being do not believe that whites are superior, and even fewer blacks who do not recognize that feeling and resent it."[2]

When I was a twenty-year-old Catholic seminarian, I volunteered to be a counselor for two weeks at a summer camp for poor kids. I felt pretty virtuous about that. The kids were so needy and so grateful for this little summer respite. One day I was walking along the road and two of the boys ran after me, wanting to walk with me. I plopped my hand on each of their heads as they joined me, and suddenly I withdrew my hand from one head. That hair was different.

There were no clean heads in that camp, not even the counselors', but my response had nothing to do with dirt. The kid was black. Like the instantaneous withdrawal response sent by the brain when we accidentally touch something red-hot, my whiteness was instinctively repulsed by blackness. Racism is an American inheritance. It is so ugly we rarely look it in the eye. The moment was for me a growth spurt accompanied by chagrin.

Crucial to the stubborn success of contemporary racism is the belief that it is no longer a problem. Crucial, too, is the refusal of whites to believe that the privileges that come with whiteness are parasitically in debt to the disadvantages our systems impose on blacks. The perquisites of the overclass are always organically linked to the deprivations of the underclass. Like mosquitoes, we are little aware of those whose blood we suck.

REALITY CHECK

Let's go into the living room and dare to meet the elephant; it's a trip not even liberals like to take. Facing mordant racism head-on with all its implications in our domestic and foreign policy is not part of the reigning liberal chic. Of course, it is a nonissue on the right. What often goes unspoken can be vicious, especially because it still operates. The malignant myth as I state it below still effectively shapes American customs and policies. So let's be blunt about this pandemic and say it out loud.

The Malignant Myth of African American Inferiority

Let's face it. The blacks don't have it. They got here in 1619 and they are still in the cellar. All immigrants have it tough. The Italians, the Irish, the Poles, the Chinese—they all started at the bottom of American economic life, but they worked their way out of it. Many of them came with little more than the clothes on their backs, but they struggled, survived, and eventually thrived. "Catholics need not apply!" was written on factory doors. The Catholics didn't whine; they made fun of those signs, writing on them, "Whoever wrote this wrote it well, for the same is written on the gates of hell!" Catholics toiled and sent their kids to school and ended up in the White House and on just about every corporate board. More recently, Laotians, Koreans, and Vietnamese came to these shores, not having even a command of our alphabet, much less our language, and suddenly they are resented (usually by neighboring blacks) for their almost instantaneous success. Even West Indian blacks are doing relatively well economically. If blacks can't make it after more than three hundred years, there is nothing wrong with America. There is something wrong with blacks.

Some gutsy scholars admit this. In 1969, Arthur Jensen wrote in the Harvard Educational Review *that the limited intellectual potential of blacks was due to genetics. William Shockley, a Nobel Prize–winning physicist, supported him by stating that intelligence is "color coded." And Harvard urbanologist Edward Banfield got right to the point: "Men accustomed to a street-corner style of life, to living of off women on welfare, and to 'hustling' are seldom willing to accept the dull routines of the 'good' job." More recently, Harvard's Richard Herrstein and President Ronald Reagan's favorite social scientist, Charles Murray, forthrightly connected race and low intelligence in their book* The Bell Curve.

And it isn't as though we haven't tried to help blacks. God knows we have! We passed civil rights legislation. Remember, too, urban renewal in 1949, community action programs in 1964, model cities in 1966, community development and urban development grants in the 1970s, and enterprise zones in the 1980s. They were all code names for helping blacks, and they all failed.

There are some exceptional blacks, of course, but overall, blacks are not very bright or highly motivated and there really isn't too much that we can do for them. They have their hands out for help, but they won't help themselves. In fact, it seems like the more we do for them, the more they turn to crime and rioting.

Thomas Jefferson professed with classical eloquence his belief that all "men" were created equal, and yet, in his hon-

esty, he admitted to a suspicion that blacks were inferior to whites in both mind and body. "Their inferiority is not the effect merely of their condition of life. . . . It is not their condition . . . but nature, which has produced the distinction . . . ." Blacks, he noted, secreted less by the kidneys and more by the glands of the skin, "which give them a very strong and disagreeable odor." They are "more ardent after their female," and love seemed with them "to be more an eager desire than a tender, delicate mixture of sentiment and sensation. Their griefs are transient . . . their existence appears to participate more of sensation than reflection."[3] (He was not, it seems, terribly put off by black women.)

Abraham Lincoln knew it too. In his 1858 campaign he made clear that he wanted to free the slaves only to get rid of them and send them back to Africa where they belong. In a speech in Charleston he put it on the line: "I am not, nor ever have been, in favor of bringing about in any way the social and political equality of the white and black races [applause]: that I am not, nor ever have been, in favor of making voters or jurors of negroes, nor of qualifying them to hold office, nor to intermarry with white people. . . . I am in favor of having the superior position assigned to the white race."[4]

The myth, thus stated, may stick in the throat of those who would rush to the "how far we have come" defense. A few diagnostic questions might coax a little honesty from white America. Here goes:

Has the white distaste for having black grandchildren diminished?

Is the black fiancé who comes to dinner as welcome as would be a Hispanic American?

Since our biology has no objections, do we find sexual attraction to very dark African Americans as natural as attraction to mulattos or to whites?

Have we dated a black person?

Do we think of the unique problems of black children when we vote?

Do we react to black skin the way we react to red or blond hair, as inconsequential variations on the human theme?

Are we less comfortable in the presence of redheaded or blond people?

Do we think that smart redheads are an exception?

Were we as children told to lock the car door when we were driving through a neighborhood with a lot of redheads, and do we carry that implicit memory in our minds?

If we were picking models for advertising, would we object if their hair was too red? (Notice the overwhelming preference for mulatto models and the paucity of really dark ones.)

And again, and crucially, are we really indifferent as to whether our children or grandchildren will be redheaded or mulatto? Really, really indifferent? (It would be argued that our hesitation is based on fear of the discrimination that will greet black children. That is not the point here. The point is this; do we, in our hearts, think of a black baby as just as huggable and cuddly as a white baby, with no hints of antipathy or negativity? If the answer is no, the reason is racism.)

*And since race affects our political consciousness, do we
understand the differences between white and black reac-
tions to the O.J. Simpson not-guilty verdict?*

Racism is a ubiquitous smog in American culture, not
limited to white against black. It is manipulated for political gain. Witness the Republican "Southern strategy," or
Richard Nixon wooing Italian American voters, telling them,
"You people work for a living!" Racism surfaces in attitudes
toward Muslims and the alleged "clash of civilizations." It
permeates immigration debates. Its furnace is fear and hatred of otherness.

CATHOLICS IN DEFAULT

To put it all too gently: Catholics in the United States have
not been leaders in the fight against racism. It's past time to
call Catholics before the bar of their own professed ideals.
Catholic social-justice teaching spawned "liberation theology," a vision based on "solidarity with victims" and "a preferential option for the poor." It has done marvels for the poor
of Latin America and has become a powerful political ideology inspiring the Latin American left.

Catholic liberation theology, not communism, is behind
the recent political triumphs on the left in Latin American
nations.

Meanwhile, back in the United States, liberation theology has had no impact on our black ghettoes. It's not a Catholic
issue here. When former presidential vice presidential candi-

date Geraldine Ferraro asked me to do a breakfast briefing for her fellow Catholic congresspersons, the issue was not black poverty. It was not the issue of black infants still dying at twice the rate of white infants or pregnant black women dying at three times the rate of pregnant white women.[5] Those would be real prolife issues. *But they are not Catholic issues.* When presidential candidate Jimmy Carter called the most prominent Catholic theologian, Father Charles Curran at Catholic University of America, he did not have racial justice in mind. These astute politicians were calling on the only issue they saw Catholics morally serious about: *abortion.*

Catholics were leaders in "white flight." An immigrant church had immigrant prejudices. While growing up in Catholic Philadelphia, we all knew what it meant when people spoke of a parish "going down." It meant the blacks were coming and the whites were running, with Catholics leading the pack. Sad to tell, but it must be told: American Catholics have never accepted black men and women as their brothers and sisters "made in the image and likeness of God," as the catechism puts it. And a tragic old story it is. Protestants led the way in the antislavery movement. Catholics (and the Missouri Synod Lutherans) "took no position on slavery."[6] (It would be a nice exercise in ecumenism for Catholics to take lessons from Muslims, who have made American blacks feel at home.)

FROM TALKING TO WALKING

What makes the Catholic defection more culpable is the fact that they know better. Clarence Thomas is a Catholic. On

this issue he would be a better one if he listened to his bishops. The United States Conference of Catholic Bishops,
never known to be a nest of radicals, put out a "pastoral letter" in 1979, "Brothers and Sisters to Us."[7] Please note: bishops never put out ideas that are not hypergrounded in the
tradition. They are not innovators or trailblazers. Here are
some of the remarkable points the bishops made:

1. Confession of Church guilt

No hedging here. "Racism is an evil that endures in our
Church," say the bishops. The Church, because of its attitude toward African Americans, has deserved to be seen as "a
white Church," "a racist institution" (!). Racism is a sin that
mocks the teaching of Jesus by saying that "some human beings are inherently superior and others essentially inferior
because of race." The "black Protestant churches" that inspired the civil rights movement should be the "model" for
Catholics. The Church has to move beyond "mere tokenism"
and push for "radical transformation" of society as well as the
Church. Most of the world's gluttonous, high-consumption
nations "are white and Christian," while "most of the world's
poor are of other races and religions."

2. Analysis of racism

Again, no naivete or pious fudging here. Indeed, Catholic
Church officials out-metaphor Chief Justice Warren Burger
in *Griggs v. Duke Power Co.*, where he said that all blacks

face "built-headwinds" and "artificial, arbitrary, and unnecessary barriers to employment." It's worse than "headwinds,"
say the bishops. "Racial identity [for blacks] is an iron curtain
barring the way to a decent life and livelihood." The poor,
and especially the black poor, are "asked to bear the heaviest
burden" in the new economy. The new racism is more subtle,
they say, but more vicious. It cannot be understood in
individual-to-individual terms. It is what Pope John Paul II
called "a structural evil." It is built into the economy, the educational system, "housing patterns": it thrives in the "attitudes and behavior of some law enforcement officials and in
the unequal availability of legal assistance" and in resistance
to systemic remedies such as "affirmative action." Accep-
tance by whites of this exploitative system that benefits them
by exploiting blacks is a "social sin," often masked and anony-
mous, but for which "each of us is responsible."

Racism weakens our entire "social fabric and [deprives]
our country of the unique contributions of many of our
citizens."

The cruelest part of socially ensconced racism is what it
does to our African American brothers and sisters and their
children. The bishops don't miss this. Our segregated and ill-
funded public schools manage to "inculcate a conviction of
inferiority." We rape the very soul of black children, ripping
out the natural hopes and dreams of childhood, and then we
blame the victim of this abuse.

In other words, this typically Catholic stress on social sin
and structural evil means that individual whites do not have
to mug blacks to get advantages. The system mugs them for

us and delivers the loot to us, as we wallow in our purloined privileges.

The brutality of racism is not alien to the allegedly "kind and gentle" American spirit. The bishops bluntly note: "Our history is littered with the debris of broken promises and treaties, as well as lynchings and massacres that almost destroyed the Indians, humiliated the Hispanics, and crushed the blacks," and "American racism is rooted in a history of slavery, peonage, economic exploitation, brutal repression, and cultural neglect." The bishops cite the United Nations' Universal Declaration of Human Rights, which demands the elimination of discrimination based on race. "None of these, unfortunately, have been ratified by our country, whereas we in America should have been the first to do so." The United Nations was born out of a recognition of interdependency on a shrinking and imperiled planet. On issues of peace and racial justice, its documents house some of the best insights of human history, including ideas of justice that were born and nurtured in the world's religions. The bishops and the popes do well to call for strengthening the UN and taking it seriously.

The bishops go on to call for practical measures like affirmative action, boycotting of racist industries, and strategies to promote "authentic full employment." They urge Catholics to develop "new forms of alternative investment, such as cooperatives, land trusts, and housing for the poor."

A JUSTICE MESSAGE M.I.A., AND THE MYSTERY OF "RECOVERING CATHOLICS"

That pastoral letter was not the voice of the religious right. It did faithfully reflect the ancient Jewish prophetic concern for the *anawim*, the despised and disempowered poor. It did revive the old Catholic social-justice preoccupation that surfaced with power now and then throughout history. The question, however, is where did it all go? Did the bishops mean what they said? Have sermons and homilies in Catholic churches been driving home this message of justice? Or have Catholics collectively trashed their social-justice traditions vis-à-vis blacks?

One bishop commented that Catholics were the second largest religious grouping in his diocese. The first largest grouping was former Catholics. These are the self-identified "recovering Catholics" found in high numbers in Unitarian churches and in churches such as the United Church of Christ—the UCC, which one wag said now means *U*sed to be *C*alled *C*atholic. Many leave the Catholic Church because of its authoritarian abuses. But others leave because they prefer the passions of justice to pelvic obsessions and because Catholic social-justice resources have for a long time been hidden away in the Catholic attic, unapplied to the needs at their doorstep.

That said, it remains ironically true that Catholic bishops outlined the key points of racial justice and injustice and the

impact that these have had on blacks and whites in these dis-
united states. They give the architectonic structure for a
fresh look at race matters in the USA: (1) the effects of
racism on whites, (2) the systemic nature of the problem and
the need for systemic remedies, and (3) the effects of victim-
hood on African American children and adults.

WHITES AS LOSERS

In lecturing on affirmative action, I take out a piece of loose-
leaf paper, saying it represents the millions who reside and
have resided in this country—the talent pool of this nation.
Jefferson said the goal of effective statecraft is to avail ourselves of all the richness and genius of all of our people.

First I fold the paper in half, rip it down the middle, and
drop one half to the floor, saying, "That half represents
women, whom we have historically consigned to *die Küche
und die Kinder* [the kitchen and the kids], and not to the halls
of power in church, state, or academe."

Next I tear off a two-inch strip and drop it to the floor,
saying these are our African Americans, left after slavery to
the social famines of ghetto life.

I tear off other strips representing Native Americans and
migrant workers and others left in the unforgiving chains of
poverty.

I end up with one sliver of paper representing white
men. But then I note that some of them are over sixty-five
and I clip that piece off the top (ageism). Others are under

thirty and have not yet paid their dues to the white male aristocracy, and I clip off part of the bottom.

There I stand, left with only a small strip of paper. This little sliver represents the pool from which we have drawn 99 percent of our Supreme Court justices, presidents, legislators, corporate heads, and church and academic leaders.

Conclusion: this is stupid. As the bishops put it, we have "deprived our country of the unique contribution of many of our citizens." For two hundred years we have had a white male monopoly, a quota system guaranteeing 90 to 100 percent of the top spots for white men—a splendid idea if 90 to 100 percent of the talent is white and male.

Lying on the floor, symbolized by torn and dropped bits of paper, may be those individuals who could discover the cure for the disease of which we may die, the inventors of alternative energy, the lost consolers and teachers and healers and those who could have been geniuses of harmonizing governance. How dumb we thought Hitler was in banishing all Jewish talent from his reich. Racism is a similarly stupid reich builder, stripping society of much of its human wealth.

If moral decency can't do it, self-interest should drive us to reform.

SYSTEMIC CURES FOR SYSTEMIC ILLS

Individuals can't create ghettoes; only societies can. Individuals—even a bunch of them—cannot double the rate of black infant death, or triple the rate of black maternal mortality, or move wealth from the bottom many to the top few, or give monopoly status to a certain race and a certain gender. Only collectively can we do mischief like that. It takes a force with roots in social myths operative from living rooms to boardrooms, a force that permeates laws and customs and combines the collaborative power of religion, money, public entertainment, opinion makers, and curriculum shapers, a force supported by the calculated indifference and complicit silence of those who are advantaged by these societal arrangements. Only when all that is in place, as the bishops said, can racism kill men, women, and babies and do it anonymously, with no individuals indictable for murder and with our sense of respectability still intact.

That's what the bishops call "social evil," and the popes call "structural evil." The complicity of popes and bishops in these evils does not make their analysis invalid.

Systemic evils like racism or militarism are so complex and engulfing that they may seem irresistible. They're not. Affirmative action might seem unwieldy "social engineering" except that it has worked. It has worked for white women in the schools of law and medicine. John Kennedy coined the term "affirmative action" and Lyndon Johnson put the muscle in it. Its primary beneficiaries were to be blacks, but it worked best for white women. (Not surprising.) Most law and medical schools have gender-balanced classes now (though that balance has not transferred out into the power arrangements in those professions), and women have done so well in these schools that in some cases there is rumbling about the need for a little affirmative action for white males.

These white male monopolies were not broken because a lot of white men were "born again" and decided in a burst of magnanimity to shed some of their monopolistic privileges. Hierarchies never divest willingly. Only governmental power could do it. And the government could do more of it.[8]

"Full employment" policies called for by the bishops might seem illusory and naive. But not according to distinguished economist Alice Rivlin, who states, "It does not seem, from an analytical point of view, that there is any magic number below which we cannot push unemployment. It is a question of the will and of choosing the right mix of politics."[9] The diversion of monies from capital-intensive but not labor-intensive military projects, a stress on investment in the social economy, on education, the environment, medical and child care, and other social needs—not just making more cars and toys for the affluent—are some of the steps toward full employment.[10]

What Pope John Paul II called "savage unbridled capitalism" is as irrational as drug addiction when it ignores the need for creativity in job creation. As economist and Nobel laureate Amartya Sen has said, global capitalism is self-defeating if it does not see the need to expand democracy, elementary education, and the opportunities of society's underdogs.

Any hope for change there? Running into a brick wall is instructive. As the irrationalities of the system grow more mani-

fest and more toxic, the bishops' idea of full employment—and
an active concern for all the workers in the global economy—
will look less wistful and more like a hard-nosed economic
necessity.

THE LIBERAL *AL DI LA* COMPLEX

When the bishops speak as just quoted, they're at their best.
When they address real-life problems here and now and
close to home, they can make a difference. Cardinal Roger
Mahoney of Los Angeles stormed into the immigration debate when the most hateful legislation was being proposed.
He said he would order his priests to disobey that law. Washington listened. The debate changed. Of course, Cardinal
Mahoney was motivated by his concern for Catholic Hispanics. His zeal is less visible for African Americans.

When religious leadership leads, and addresses real-life
problems, as it did in the abolition of slavery and the civil
rights movement, history turns a corner.

Permit me to dream a wild dream. Maybe bishops and
other religious leaders could cure liberals of their *al di la* disease. *Al di la* is Italian for "out there in the distant beyond."
Liberals, Catholic or not, are drawn to problems *al di la* and
not at their doorstep. This allows us to ignore more local issues, issues that could indeed summon our passions and
commitment if they were at a comfortable remove. It's easier
to direct moral concern abroad than to visit our home-grown
ghettoes like North Philadelphia or the South Bronx, or the
commercially dead zones of Los Angeles, Chicago, or At-

lanta, where social decay is a vortex that swallows people. But in this dream of mine I see a new model for liberals emerging. I see Archbishop Tutu, and Gandhi, and Mother Jones, and Nelson Mandela, and Martin Luther King Jr., and Dorothy Day becoming the models for liberals. A dream? Yes, it might be, but to adapt the words of the Irish poet Yeats, tread softly if you would tread upon that dream.

THE PERILS OF VICTIMHOOD

American racism is a mutant that cheats death by changing. The 1960s were the best of times and the worst of times for American racism. On the cheery side, civil rights legislation was passed. As Professor Derrick Bell says, there was glory for many whites in those days, "when they could jet-ride [to the] South and walk arm-in-arm with Martin and the others through the streets of some dusty Southern town and sing the songs that equated freedom and brotherhood, suggesting that the time for both was at hand."[11] Antiracism was chic. To oppose crusty Bull Connor and his vile-mouthed mobs was to feel noble on the cheap.

There is a wispy quality to any "chic." The chic of today is the banality of tomorrow. Social problems, however, are made of sterner stuff and are scarcely jostled by temporary episodes of indignation. Short-term indignation can stimulate important legislation and stir the hearts of some judges, but it cannot "change the system," with its deep and gripping roots.

The 1960s was a glory time for African Americans also.

As Arthur Ashe said, blacks had been "hemmed in by segregation, physically threatened by police and the Ku Klux Klan [which were sometimes the same, no doubt]." As a result, says Ashe, "we were a dependent, intimidated people."[12] Suddenly there was a heroic moment, with black spirit rising. Martin Luther King Jr., a Nobel laureate; the Southern Christian Leadership Conference (SCLC); boycotts of lunch counters; dignified nonviolent marches; a blending of Gandhi with the ancient Hebrew prophets—all pulled the respectability mask off the ugly face of racism. But this heady moment passed, as it was not sustained by whites or blacks. As Arthur Ashe saw it, 1965 was the peaking of black moral leadership.

Of course whites could say, "We gave you the unanimous decisions of *Brown v. Board of Education*, the Civil Rights Act of 1964, and the Voting Rights Act of 1965. What more do you expect?" The civil rights movement was effectively over. Racism mutated and increased its power because resistance to it was no longer "in."

Many blacks escaped poverty but abandoned the old neighborhoods, leaving "the poorer, less-educated strata to fend for themselves without the leadership and guidance that more fortunate blacks had often provided."[13] The success of some blacks reinforced the right-wing myth that the others could make it if they were not so shiftless and unready to embrace the American dream. Now our liberal souls were freer to turn to more pressing issues, like feminism, ecology, and militarism without having to take note of how racism infects all three of these crucial causes and crises. Left-wing could now join right-wing in the enduring American sin of denial.

Some bleeding-heart religious liberals do not bleed enough. They have a help-and-run hierarchical approach to victims, moving to new victims when the old victims get partly to their feet. They don't, as Rita Nakashima Brock says, "hang in there for long-term mutual transformation, because they would have to make themselves deeply vulnerable, rather than helpful." And they often prefer helpful.

STIGMA

My parents arrived from Ireland in 1929 with six children, walking right into the teeth of the Depression. They never had to go on "relief," as welfare was then called, and they were proud of that. Why can't blacks do the same?

My parents, on arrival, were almost penniless but rich in another way. They had whiteness for starters. On top of that they had never been stripped of their culture. While welcoming American opportunities, they were critical of the cruelties of American culture. My mother's father came briefly to America in the 1860s and returned to poor Ireland, saying, "America is no country to grow old in." My mother's use of the term "American" was usually pejorative, signifying superficiality and immaturity. The British starved the Irish, but they never succeeded in making them hate themselves. The British oppressors did not achieve *stigma*, the capstone of successful oppression. We did achieve it with African Americans. And it endures.

When I published a book some years ago, I was interviewed by a young African American reporter for a Madison, Wisconsin, radio station. The fifteen-minute interview was stellar . . . and a too-rare experience for an author. She had read the book and pushed me on all its main premises. When she finished, I said, "You are really good!" She smiled and said, "Yes, I know I am good, but I didn't always know it. When I went to Edgewood College, an all-girls Catholic college, I was scared. I was convinced that all these white girls were smarter than me and I kept quiet. A couple of the nun professors would not let me be quiet. They kept pressing me for answers, and to my amazement I kept having the answers. There was a great moment in my life when I went home, looked in the mirror, and shouted: 'You are really smart!' After that, nothing was ever the same."

I had tears in my eyes when she finished. She did not.

Dick Gregory in his heyday was a great comedian because he was also a gifted tragedian. I heard him talk to a largely white audience at Catholic University of America. He told a story about his grandmother's memories of slavery. She remembered the story of a slave woman who had to give up her children for immediate sale at birth. The rule was that only if the child was deformed could she keep her baby. After having two children taken from her like this, she then prayed that when she became pregnant, her child would be "deformed."

When I heard Gregory tell this story to the large university audience, he paused at this point, and that distinctive silence that attends the hearing of some horror gripped the entire audience in the stillness of shock. Gregory broke the silence to comment that if whites would understand blacks ("us niggers" in Gregory's parlance) they should think about that prayer for a deformed baby.

The story, however, was not yet finished. The woman's next child was born, and it was seriously deformed. When the baby was held up for her to see, she looked at its twisted body and said, "Thank God!" The silence became painfully deep as Gregory urged his white audience to "think about *that* prayer."

Stigma has sordid and tragic roots. "Niggerization" is the sad term social scientists have used to describe it. Dick Gregory explained why he called his first book *Nigger*. Some words are demonic and can capture a whole history of venom and hate. "Nigger" is one of those words. Black parents dread the moment when their happy toddler first hears that word and begins to catch the insult it contains. It is the beginning of the assault on the young child's personality core. And so Dick Gregory explained that he chose that title so that when his children first heard the terrible word, they would say, "Hey, cool, somebody's talking about my daddy's book!" Here Gregory was comedian, tragedian, and exorcist. He was driving out the devil that infuses a single word.

Stigma is deadly poison. It strips the ego of its protective covering. It can produce despair, a sapping of hope and thus of ambition and drive. With that job done, how easy it is for the victimizers to blame their victim. How easy, too, for many blacks to buy the "hard work" theory—i.e., anyone can make it if he or she really tries. In reality, blacks do work harder. In

1998, the average middle-income, married-couple African American family with children worked 489 more hours per year than a comparable white family. The black family had to work 12 more weeks than the average white family to maintain middle-class status.[14] Still, a recent study by the University of Minnesota shows the "surprising" result that 81 percent of nonwhites see effort and hard work, not a rigged and white-dominated system, as important in explaining white advantages.[15]

AN EPIC OF IRONY

African Americans put this country on its feet. Profits from the slave trade "allowed the infant American society to burst into international economic competition."[16] In the antebellum period of the nineteenth century, "slave-grown cotton was the leading export of the United States. It paid for the import of products and capital that fueled the national economy." In 1860, the value of slaves was three times the amount that had been invested in manufacturing and railroads combined. Slaves produced rum, rice, cotton, tobacco, hemp, and other goods. According to Gloria Albrecht, "The entire U.S. society was enmeshed in the economics of slavery."[17]

African Americans have enriched the culture, the sciences, and the arts. The black civil rights movement advanced not only their cause but the rights of all citizens, and provided the rhetoric and inspiration for other liberation movements for women and sexual minorities. Studies show that blacks are among those who are "most likely to support the interests of poor and lower-working-class people." [18] They are a resource for the development of a national conscience.

Black slaves had Christianity shoved down their throats. It was not their religion. It was not their culture. At first, their "owners" agonized over whether the Africans were human enough for baptism. When it was decided that they were, they were given a carefully monitored version of the Gospel, stressing obedience and compliance. But the illiterate slaves saw through it. With none of the tools of modern biblical studies, they found the recently rediscovered liberatory message of biblical history. They violated rules forbidding slave gatherings to discuss the implications of what they were hearing about this interesting God of the Christians who would lead slaves out of thralldom and into a promised land.

The masters monitored their slaves' worship services, in implicit recognition that the Gospel might be seditious. So the slaves developed what came to be called "the down-front sermon." In a loud voice that would reach the monitor at the back, the preacher preached obedience and hard work, but then in a lower voice cloaked in dialect, he delivered the down-front message to eager ears that they, too, were made "in the image of God," that their babies were as precious to this biblical God as the master's children, and that owning— not being—the slave was the ultimate sin. They were given a corrupted Christianity, and they had the genius to reform it.

One of the greatest sins of white racism is the absence of gratitude for the gifts we have among us.

CURATIVE CLOSENESS

Racism is not inscribed in our genes. It can fade like the morning mist. My son Tom married a dark-skinned African American, Karen Hunt. In my Irish background, a mixed marriage used to be one where a white Catholic married a white Protestant, and in Ireland it even extended to when a Donegal man married a girl from Mayo, an adjacent county! It was all tabooed miscegenation and socially disapproved. Now, back to Tom and Karen. To top off Karen's skin color, another note was added to this "guess who's coming to dinner" package: she and Tom converted to Islam.

You might ask how this went over with my born-in-Ireland Catholic family, some now in their nineties. Report: when my four mixed-race Muslim grandchildren arrive at my family members' doorsteps they fully expect to be adored. And they are. The family complaints I hear are that there are not enough visits from this family and not enough pictures sent.

Contact can be a bias solvent, and love removes veils of inherited ignorance. There's hope in that for all the nasty isms that hobble our affections, limit our lives, and undermine our peace.

4

War Is for Dummies
(Antidotes in Lost Traditions)

Mahatma Gandhi was asked one time, "What do you think of Western Civilization?" He replied, "That would be a great idea!"

The historian Howard Zinn said, "One third of our military budget would provide water and sanitation facilities for the billion people worldwide who have none. Let us be a more modest nation. The modest nations of the world don't face the threat of terrorism. Let us pull back from being a military superpower and become a humanitarian superpower. Then we, and everyone else, will be more secure."

I remember the day I took my son Danny to visit the beautiful lagoon off Lake Michigan in Milwaukee just before he died at age ten. I had been driving past it every day going to school, thinking serious thoughts to be sure, but not looking. Danny looked. He saw the beautiful mallard ducks and waterfowl of every kind, and he grabbed my leg and shouted, "Daddy, look!" I see that as Danny's valedictory ad-

*dress to me and to the world—the plea he left to us
who are more retarded than he. We don't look. We
don't look at this generous earth that has been given
to us, an earth that we are progressively wrecking.
We don't look at the hungry of the world. We don't
look at what we are doing when we unleash Shake-
speare's "dogs of war."*

WAR STORIES

Michael Walzer tells us of an incident in World War I. The
year was 1914. The Germans and the French had been
shooting at one another. One side or the other realized that it
was Christmas Day, and so they put down their weapons and
started singing carols. The other side joined them, and they
came together singing and sharing drinks in the no-man's-
land between their lines. When this had ended, they dutifully
returned to killing one another.[1]

A similar story comes to us from World War II. American
soldiers were guarding German prisoners, with rifles at the
ready. Four of the Germans who comprised a trained quartet
began humming a tune. Within a few minutes, the tense at-
mosphere changed. The rifles were dropped to the ground,
and with these weapons still lying around, both sides started
to hum together, share cigarettes, and show snapshots of
loved ones at home. The mythic "image of the enemy" was no
match for a song. Eros was stronger than Mars. Then the
commanding officer arrived and indignantly reinvoked the
myth. Back came the rifles and the fiction was forced back in

place. Reality had broken through for a moment. The reality
was that these soldiers on both sides were victims, citizens
enthralled by military fictions into a false consciousness
wrapped around them like a noose. The noose had loosened
for a lucid moment, and they saw "the enemy" as flesh and
blood, human comrades trapped temporarily in a madness
not of their making.[2]

Let's travel back to the hearty old days of warring, when
the mayhem was highly ritualized. In the early fourteenth
century in Europe, the standard operating procedure for organized killing had not changed for five hundred years. Soldiers showed up on a field, dressed in their proper colors (so
you could tell friend from foe). Then they went at one another until one side prevailed or until both sides collapsed
and those left standing went home to spin the event as best
they could.

In 1346, however, things changed, or rather one side
changed the ritual. The French nobles arrived for battle at
Crécy bedecked in their normal fashion. The British, however, had come upon the longbow and realized that they did
not need fancy knights to use it. They trained peasant longbowmen and mowed the French down from a safe distance.

One would think that such an onslaught would focus the
minds of some of the French military geniuses. But no. The
"military mind" is not a quick study. Ten years later, at
Poitiers, the French once again rode to their deaths in a hail
of arrows. Worse yet, the point was still ungrasped, and in
1415 they did the same stupid thing at Agincourt. It was
then that it began to dawn on them that this five-hundred-

year protocol of charging knights was no longer a winning strategy.[3]

We might smirkingly view these debacles as relics of times past, not something that would be at home in our sophisticated modernity. But wait! Let us move from Crécy, Poitiers, and Agincourt to Iraq in 2003, and what do we see?

We see American forces arriving dressed and equipped for World War II. But, oops! No Nazi army awaits them. No observant enemy dressed in appropriate uniforms and using the old weapons and playing by the old rules. How cruel! A rules change with no prior notification. So, there we were, like the French at Crécy, carefully uniformed and easily identifiable targets. The noise of our military equipment could be heard from half a mile away as resistance forces decide whose turn it was to push the detonator. Arrogance is the firstborn of dumbness. "Bring 'em on!" said our president. And on they did come!

We had tried this old-time warfare in the jungles of Vietnam and finally had to scramble out in defeat. Still, our doltish leaders would give it another try in the Middle East. What we were missing was that the enemy now swims invisibly in the sea of the populace, surfacing at will and deciding which of our cumbersome machines would next be blasted into smithereens. The Iraqi people, who do not enjoy being invaded, do enjoy an unmatchable trinity of strategic advantages: *invisibility*, *versatility*, and *patience*. War had mutated but our dummy leaders had not. The slow attrition of guerrilla warfare commenced.

Mikhail Gorbachev offered us friendly advice when he

noted that business is now the new battlefield. Similarly friendly was a Chinese official who commented on our second Iraq war: "You invade oil-rich countries: we simply buy the oil. It's cheaper. More efficient. No one gets hurt."

War demands dimness of wit and mental gimmicks to avoid reality-contact. Without myths it just won't work. We need a fictive "image of the enemy," since if we saw the human beings these "enemies" are—people like us, full of hopes and foibles—we could not easily kill them. There are many examples in battles that show just how artificial the myths of war are, how the "image of the enemy" is an artifact, a concoction of deceptions.

DUMBNESS AS A GROUP ACTIVITY

It is not just the soldiers who indulge in the temporary insanity of bellicosity. To rev up a society for war, collective distortion is job one. "In 1942 and again in 1966 respondents were asked to choose from a list of adjectives those that best described the people of Russia, Germany, and Japan. In 1942 the first five adjectives chosen to characterize both Germans and Japanese (enemies) were warlike, treacherous, and cruel, none of which appeared among the first five describing the Russian (allies)." By 1966 the Germans and Japanese were wonderful, attractive people, and it was now the Russians who were "warlike, treacherous, and cruel." [4]

War is a mutant, changing constantly—from charging knights in bright clanging armor to longbowmen with their arrows, from uniformed soldiers in armored planes and vehi-

cles to skulking guerrilla warriors. Such changes show that
the mode of war is an artificial construct of human imagination. We make up different ways of doing it. This should raise
questions. Why not have a duel between the two leaders of
the countries involved and agree to abide by the result? Is
that any sillier or dumber than having armies of coerced citizens from the lower economic classes out slaughtering one
another while gouging and wrecking the rest of nature, and
then deciding to abide by those results? What does slaughter
really prove? And how do you really "win" a debacle?

HOLY WAR

Religion and violence is a horrid mix. Religion is powerful
and warriors need power. So when we go to war we bring our
gods along. *Gott mit uns* (God is with us) was stamped on the
belt buckles of Hitler's troops. *Deus vult* (it is God's will) was
shouted by the Crusaders as they embarked on slaughter.
The Confederacy invoked "the favor and guidance of the
Almighty God" as they girded for the Civil War, and took as
their motto *Deo vindice* (God will avenge). The Union soldiers had a different take on God's loyalties. "The Battle
Hymn of the Republic" was an epic of pious slaughter; the
march of "Onward Christian Soldiers" to battle was seen as
"the glory of the coming of the Lord": "As [Jesus] died to
make men holy, let us die to make men free / While God is
marching on!" In World War II the home-front folks sang,
"Praise the Lord and pass the ammunition." And then there
is George W. Bush speaking piously to his heavenly father be-

fore inflicting "shock and awe" on the people of Iraq. In an unguarded but revealing moment he called his mission "a crusade," the holy war term used by Eisenhower to describe World War II. It is not just Muslims who paint the horrors of jihad and war in sacral hues. Our English word "war" is just as laden with religious connotations as the Muslim "jihad" is with some Muslims. Thus we call American-soldier victims "heroes," noble sacrifices, and we put religious symbols on their graves. This is perverted religion and warriors major in it.

When it comes to war, religion has often been more of a problem than a solution. In a study of thirty-eight ongoing conflicts in the world today, religion is listed as at least partially causative in sixteen of them.[5] Since religion is so active in warfare and a powerful motivator in any context, we dare not ignore it.

Catholics have been neck high in the war business. Indeed, one of the rare instances of Catholic thought going mainstream and becoming a staple of international discourse is what Jonathan Schell calls "the Catholic just-war theory."[6] This was both good and bad. On the good side, drawing from Greeks and Romans who saw the need to do some taming of the passions of war, Catholics polished up a set of criteria: war had to do more good than harm (the test of proportionality); you needed a "just cause" and a "right intention"; war had to be declared by legitimate authority; and it had to spare noncombatants. It would be hard to find a war that passed all those noble tests, but the well-intentioned goal was to put some limit on the lawless juggernaut that war tends to become. Properly understood, as explained in the following pages, the venerable just-war theory can be a gateway to peacemaking.

The problem, of course, is that making rules for war is a bit like making rules for an orgy: neither activity is very patient of restraint.

A downside was that "just-war theory" put war and justice in the same bed and made the conception of war seem normal, inevitable—just one of those things. In the famous words of the Prussian officer Karl von Clausewitz, it was "a continuation of policy . . . by other means." As Barbara Ehrenreich says, this tragically faulty view implies that war involves "the kind of clearheaded deliberation one might apply to a game of chess . . . no more disturbing and irrational than, say, a difficult trade negotiation—except perhaps to those who lay dying on the battlefield."[7]

We have defanged war, making it seem so respectable that we can use it in all sorts of innocent and lovely contexts: "the war on poverty," "the war on cancer," "the war on illiteracy," etc. We wouldn't talk about raping those problems or doing a "gang bang" on them because those activities, though they go on, are acknowledged as no-no's. Not so war. War can even be armchair spectator entertainment. It is fine for people to become "Civil War buffs," or "Revolutionary War buffs," but if people were to announce themselves as "necrophilia buffs" or "child abuse buffs," their perverted absorption in such human disasters would raise eyebrows.

War is so sewn into the sinews of our imaginations that it crops up in the gentlest of contexts. Walter Sullivan, in his prize-winning book *We Are Not Alone*, writes beautifully of the intelligence of dolphins. He alludes to the possibility that we may someday be able to communicate extensively with them and even train them for complex tasks. This tantalizing prospect took him immediately to war. Dolphins could be used "by one government to scout out the submarines of another . . . to smuggle bombs into enemy harbors . . . serve on underwater demolition teams . . . [be taught to] sneak up on hostile submarines and shout something into the listening gear." He worries, however, that the dolphins might demur, that "they might prove to be pacifists."[8] Their nonhuman consciousness might be less amenable to truculence. Our species should be slow to speak of descending to the level of animals. As Erich Fromm says, the human being "is the only mammal who is a large-scale killer and sadist." He cites evidence that if we had the same aggressiveness as the chimpanzees in their natural setting, our world would be a kinder place by far.[9]

A LITTLE HOPE, PLEASE!

Okay. We have a retardation problem. We look on war as normal and our best bet when the chips are down. On top of that, when we go to war we assume God is on our side, that we are the righteous and the other guys are evil. We are so madly in love with war that we will starve our kids to build bombs. The United States spends over $30 million an hour, around $10,000 a second, on kill-power, while states go bankrupt and over 40 million men, women, and children are with-

out health insurance, teachers are underpaid, and our infrastructure crumbles. Crazy? Quite! And that's our problem.

Religions helped create the problem by blessing the
tanks and God-blessing America as it stormed into its foreign
invasions. Surprisingly, religion can help demythologize war.
And in a theocracy like the United States, it absolutely has to
help. "Theocracy"? Too strong a term for secular, sophisticated America? Not at all. Kevin Phillips's book *American
Theocracy* is just one recognition of this fact. "No other contemporary Western nation shares the religious intensity"
shown in the United States, he writes, with "its concomitant
proclamation that Americans are God's chosen people and
nation. George W. Bush has averred this belief on many
occasions." [10]

In recent polls, 94 percent of Americans believe in God,
75 percent believe in Satan, and around 80 percent see
heaven and hell as postmortem realities. And 83 percent believe in the literal virgin birth of Jesus, even though Bible
scholars see this as metaphoric. Condescending sneers at
older theocracies are quite unbecoming a fundamentalist nation like this.

RELIGIONS AS WORKSHOPS

Imagination and memory: those are the tools religion brings
to an exorcism of the naive belief that war is the ultimate
sacrament of our safety.

First to history: Catholic Christianity has lived through
wars and rumors of wars since it began. There are lessons

there that "the feeble mind"[11] of this nation needs to learn. Taking the Catholic Christian story as one part of human history, we can see two messages: (1) ideals and really smart ideas can be born and then lost again, and (2) war is dumb, very dumb, and getting dumber. These are not just lessons for Catholics: these are lessons for humanity. Religions are, after all, classical and paradigmatic examples both of human foibles and of human possibilities.

THE BREAKTHROUGH

We are all in debt to ancient Israel for this insight: war is dumb. It messes up more than it fixes. The early Hebrews took the next logical step and said it was also immoral. The great Jewish theologian Abraham Heschel states the dramatic fact that the early Israelites were the first people in history to regard a nation's reliance on force as evil.

It wasn't as though they hadn't given violent force a chance. It wasn't a romantic and wild idealism that brought them to this disenchantment with arms. They had been a hearty warring folk who imagined their God as a ferocious warrior. (God talk always reflects deeply held convictions.) "The Lord is a warrior . . . majestic in strength" who lets loose his "fury" and unleashes the "blast" of divine "anger" (Exod. 15:3–8). No peacenik, this God. And not much of a start for a peace movement!

After a long history of bloodletting, however, they concluded that it didn't work. They had their "Duh!" moment. "Neither by force of arms nor by brute strength" would the people be saved (Zech. 4:6). With stunning confidence they predicted that other nations that rely on force will get the message themselves: "The nations shall see and be ashamed of all their might" (Mic. 7:16). Those who boasted of the then state-of-the-art weapons, horses and chariots, would "totter and fall" (Ps. 20:7–8). "The song of the military" would be silenced and fortified cities would become ruins (Isa. 25:5–12). You cannot build "Zion in bloodshed" (Mic. 3:10). (Modern Israel, of course, is still trying to do that and proving the old prophets' point: it doesn't work.)

Isaiah acknowledged that this breakthrough idea is "a new thing" and a hard sell. He blurted with realistic impatience, "Can you not perceive it!?" (Isa. 43:16–20). But it was a vision based not on wifty dreaming but on the experience of violence. As the Christian Paul put it: "If you go on fighting one another, tooth and nail, all you can expect is mutual destruction" (Gal. 5:15). The message is painfully relevant today, in Iraq, Afghanistan, Israel, Chechnya, East Timor, and beyond. The deeply ingrained confidence of humans in violence-as-savior leaves nations impaled on the same fatal illogic of tit-for-tat reprisal that inspired and consumed the Hatfields and the McCoys.

Christians accepted the peace message from their parent, Israel, and ran with it for three centuries. At the same time Virgil was singing of "arms and the man," Jesus was saying in a violent situation: "Put up your sword. All who take the sword die by the sword" (Matt. 26:52). For a time, this was taken as the law of Christ: "Christ in disarming Peter disarmed every soldier," said Tertullian.[12]

As late as the year 304 the eloquent Christian Lactantius was saying that "participation in warfare therefore will never be legitimate for a just man."[13] Thus the chorus of early Christianity.

But then this long peace protest got waylaid and disappeared with a terrible suddenness. At the fringes of the Roman Empire order broke down as the Pax Romana fractured; battles raged and Christians leaped into the fray. Along came Constantine, who sort of converted to Christianity. It is better said that Constantine converted Christianity to him. After Constantine became an eclectic Christian, Christians moved from persecution to preferment, and it was a heady wine that sent them reeling. The sword suddenly was a friend and no one was about to beat it into a plowshare. Theologians rationalized the change, saying that Constantine's triumphs were the work of God to serve that other work of God, the Church. Nice! A shotgun marriage joined Jesus to state-sponsored violence.

What a full circle Jesus had come! The Roman Empire killed him; now he was married to it. Constantine would now conquer under the sign of Jesus's cross. Jesus got a new career as a warlord. A fourth-century bishop of Nisibis reported with awe that in response to prayer, Jesus had routed the Persians by sending "a cloud of mosquitoes and gnats to tickle the trunks of the enemy's elephants and the nostrils of his horses." The new Jesus was not just tough but versatile. Christian abhorrence and avoidance of military service faded so far that by 416 you had to prove you were a Christian to serve in the Roman army!

To tame the born-again beast of war, Christians writers such as Augustine and Ambrose rushed to gather the seeds of the "just-war theory" from Greek and Roman writers. Peace and peacemaking was more for the City of God, not the City of Man, Augustine said, and it certainly wasn't the City of God that he saw out his window. He baptized state-sponsored violence (war), saying in terms more redolent of a library than a battlefield, "Love does not exclude wars of mercy waged by the good." [14] That blessed the illusion of all warriors. They are always doing good, whether shouldering "the white man's burden," as Kipling saw it; assuming *une mission civilatrice*, as French empire builders would have it; "promoting the revolution of the proletariat," the Soviet form of mercy; or bringing "freedom and democracy" to oil-rich lands with loving acts of "shock and awe." Thank you, Augustine! Intellectuals like you always come through with the specious shields the warriors need. And so it came to pass that the nascent "just-war theory" dissolved into a bloody and sordid dew, failing its first test. Christendom became a cauldron of violence as the so-called barbarians arrived.

Violence is inherently escalatory. In subsequent centuries, there were well-meaning, almost comical efforts to stem the tide of violence. The "Truce of God" was instituted in the tenth century. The terms of the "truce" are oh so revealing. It banned all killing for several months around the feast of Easter, for the four weeks before Christmas, and on all Fridays, Sundays, and holy days, of which at that time there were many. Church properties and the clergy were always to be exempt from violence (the clergy, after all, were making the rules!). Also exempt: peasants, pilgrims, agricultural animals, and olive trees. From age twelve on, everyone was bound to take an oath to obey the Truce and, with bizarre irony, to take up arms and kill those who would not conform.[15]

I have just stated the terms of the Truce in full purity. Purity lapsed, as can be seen from the abridged form of the oath taken by Robert the Pious (a designation suggesting that he was a cut above his peers!); Robert, you will see, was a master at equivocation and truly gifted in cover-your-tracks exception making. "I will not burn houses or destroy them, unless there is a knight inside. I will not root up vines. [Note: no exceptions here; Robert was simply not a vine-rooter-upper.] I will not attack noble ladies nor their maids nor widows or nuns, unless it is their fault. (One senses it frequently was their fault.) From the beginning of Lent to the end of Easter I will not attack an unarmed Knight."[16] Thus the moral resolve of the pious Robert.

As one historian observed: "The disease was too radical to respond to such first aid."[17]

The violence that could not be subdued was diverted into the Crusades. Lopping off heads replaced turning the other cheek. The slaughterous fury of these wars against the "infidels" showed how dangerous saints can be when they turn to arms. Note John Calvin's dictum: "No heed is to be paid to humanity when the honor of God is at stake."[18] Calvin's dictum is not dead. Today, much of the Crusading spirit lingers in the religious right with their zeal for war. Theirs is the big-bang theory of the return of Jesus, to be heralded by a colossal war which only the blessed will survive. Their current love of Israel is based on the idea that Jesus will touch down there following the conflagration. At that point the only good Jew will be a converted one; the rest will have been scorched into ashes. The lack of horror at and even enthusiasm for war in many Christians is the residue of a Christian history drenched in blood. The avoidance of war is not a "family value" for the Christian right.

So, in sum, here are the lessons of this brief history: the ancient Jews saw the dumbness of war and the possibility of peacemaking replacing war-making; Christians grabbed it, held on to it for a time, and then dumped it and joined the war addicts. The lessons for the rest of humanity: we are congenitally in love with war; we keep proving that war does not work and we keep not getting the message. Perhaps there is no area in which humanity is more obtuse.

And yet there is hope.

The dumbness of war is beginning to show with a new clarity, and the ancient Jewish and early Christian idea of nonviolent resistance is reviving as hard proof of its practicality mounts.

PEACEMAKING VS. MAKING WAR

Peacemaking isn't dumb. Nonviolent resistance works better than slaughter. Almost bloodlessly, dictators such as Ferdinand Marcos and at least seven Latin American despots have been driven out. As Walter Wink notes: "In 1989–90 alone fourteen nations underwent nonviolent revolutions. . . .

Britain's Indian colony of three hundred million people was liberated non-violently at a cost of about 8,000 lives. . . . France's Algerian colony of about ten million was liberated by violence and it cost almost one million lives."[19] Do the numbers.

Power in our day is being redefined on the ground. The United States, the alleged "last remaining superpower," lost its first war in Vietnam and now, for the first time in history, it is losing two wars simultaneously, in Iraq and Afghanistan. So, the "bully on the block," as Colin Powell described us in 1992, is getting beat up by the little kids. As Duane Elgin says in his hope-filled book *Promise Ahead: A Vision of Hope and Action for Humanity's Future*, our pretensions of invulnerability are illusory.

Military power, even "superpower" military power, is being embarrassed and examples of successful nonviolent modes of resistance are multiplying. Alternatives to military slaughter are being tested and proved. Our big nuclear biceps meant nothing in Vietnam, Iraq, or Afghanistan. September 11, 2001, proved that a handful of men with nothing more than box-cutters and penknives as weapons could destroy the Twin Towers and the Pentagon, symbols of American economic and military strength. This signaled the end of nation-versus-nation warfare as in World War II. As Karen Armstrong says, "it was an attack against the United States, but it was a warning to all of us in the First World."[20] It made us aware of our brand-new nakedness and a raw vulnerability. If our policies inspire hatred around the world, and they do—see *Why Do People Hate America?* by Ziauddin Sardar and Merryl Wyn Davies—the angry of the world have the means to get at us. The national security strategy of the United States in 2002 admitted that America is now threatened less by conquering states than by failing ones, less by fleets and armies than by catastrophic technologies in the hands of the embittered few.

A recent estimate by information warfare specialists at the Pentagon reveals how vulnerable developed nations are. The study estimated that a well-prepared attack by fewer than thirty computer whizzes with a budget of less than $10 million could bring the United States to its knees, shutting down everything from electric power grids to air traffic control centers.

This is not mere theoretical speculation. The *New York Times* (May 29, 2007, page A1) reported that after Russian outrage about the removal of a bronze statue of a World War II–era Soviet soldier from a park in Tallinn, Estonia, a cyberattack ensued which came close to shutting down the country's digital infrastructure. This monstrous genie is out of the bottle.

Also, in no way can we adequately protect our 1,000 harbor channels, our 3,700 passenger and cargo terminals, the 7 million cargo containers moving in and out of all parts of our ports, factories, and refineries; we cannot protect all our fish farms and megafarms, our chemical plants and nuclear energy facilities. To penetrate any of this is to penetrate us and they are all penetrable. The idea of protected borders has become obsolete. A single rifle in the hands of two men changed life for twenty-two days in the nation's capital and in

Virginia in 2002. Mere hundreds of trained and motivated persons could paralyze our nation, with catastrophic effect on all commerce.

Atomic devices, which fit in a suitcase and can be easily hidden in huge cargo containers, are now technically feasible. Angering nations by our aggressive policies motivates those with access to use them, and—*your attention please!*—we should anticipate their use in the United States if present trends continue. Our unmatchable kill-power is becoming Confederate money that can't be spent. Israel has the kill-power to pulverize the entire Middle East, but Israelis cannot ride a bus or dine out without fear. Russia with its arsenal could reduce all of Chechnya to radioactive dust, but it can't prevail there or live in peace at home. As with brash teenagers who reluctantly learn that bulging biceps do not guarantee success, nations on military steroids are being taught a lesson.

CATHOLIC JUST-WAR THEORY
TO THE RESCUE

Let's face it, Catholics helped create the monstrous myth of war as salvific. The "Catholic just-war theory" implied (as it was usually interpreted) that war is fine if only certain amenities are observed. Taken seriously and properly understood, it's an undiscovered gem. If the theory were called instead the "justifiable slaughter theory" or the "justifiable violence theory," it would have had the merit of being honest. Maybe the slaughter and the human and ecological destruction we are contemplating are justifiable, but at least we would be honest in admitting what it is we are justifying. It would be language without legerdemain.

Indeed, war as described in the United Nations charter—collective police action in response to real aggression verified as such by the community of nations—is a defensible form of state-sponsored violence for the foreseeable future. Its necessity will diminish if and when the nascent science of peacemaking matures. Unfortunately, many of the signatories who are treaty-bound to the United Nations charter (especially the United States) have trashed the civilizing, restraining moral insight contained in that charter and returned to the barbarous vigilante warfare now called "preemptive."

The popularity of "just-war theory" is understandable because if war is not "just," it is a murderous massacre. And so the "just-war theory" is deceptively trotted out in various warped forms to justify the war du jour. It has become the refuge of scoundrels, the pious mask of brutality. Expressions like "collateral damage" (now so common as to be a movie title) and claims of a "just cause" for war are related to the historical apparatus and jargon of "just-war theory"(also called JWT). That said, it has become the coin of the realm in international war talk, and we must employ it and show its subversive peacemaking power when properly understood. Let the real "just-war theory" stand up.

Surprise! Taken seriously, the JWT would prove that all of the recent U.S. wars have been immoral and therefore nothing more than organized murder.

The JWT had an honest birthing: it was born of the

recognition that war is a horror and any defense of it bears a huge burden of proof. It set up a series of six tests, and for a war to be "just" it must pass not one or two but all. Otherwise, the "war" is a massacre, a state-sponsored slaughterfest.

1. A just cause

Defense is the only "just cause." If a war is to get oil, more territory, to wreak vengeance for past perceived offenses, or presented as a preemptive attack on possible future threats, it is not a just war and has flunked the first test. It was for this reason that the Nuremberg trials treated preemptive war as a war crime. It was for this reason, with the fresh memory of Hitler's preemptive war, that the United Nations charter to which the United States is bound by treaty forbade preemptive wars and permitted state-sponsored violence (war) when nations react collectively within UN guidelines. The term "preemptive war" is a mask for aggressive wars and vigilante wars. President George W. Bush lapsed into honesty when he called it a "crusade."

Richard Falk writes, "World War II ended with the historic understanding that recourse to war between states could no longer be treated as a matter of national discretion, but must be regulated to the extent possible through rules administered by international institutions. The basic legal framework was embodied in the UN charter, a multilateral treaty largely crafted by American diplomats and legal advisers. [There's a bit of irony!] Its essential feature was to entrust the Security Council with administering prohibition of recourse to international force (Article 2, Section 4) by states except in circumstances of self-defense, which itself was restricted to responses to a prior 'armed attack' (Article 51) and only then until the Security Council had the chance to review the claim."[21]

This meant that state-sponsored violence, like violent police action, may be necessary in extremis, but it should be in a communitarian context, hemmed in by legal restraints. Police cannot make preemptive attacks on potential trouble spots in the city.

2. Declaration by competent authority

War can only be justified if it is waged to protect the common good, and the government is, by definition, the prime caretaker of the common good. Corporations or gangs can't declare war, though in reality that is just what tends to happen. Our splendid Constitution saw the danger and said that it is the prerogative of Congress "to declare war" and to "provide for the common Defence." President Truman led the trashing of this provision of the Constitution when he attacked Korea without a declaration of war, and no president has honored it ever since. The cop-out now in vogue is for a supine Congress to pass a "resolution" handing over the war-making powers to the president—exactly what the Founders did not want.

The Congress-as-patsy syndrome is not the only culprit in this defection. A wimpy citizenry, beguiled by bread and circuses, can't even produce a whimper of protest. As Anne

Frank wrote, "I don't believe that only governments and capitalists are guilty of aggression. Oh no, the little man is just as keen on it, for otherwise the people of the world would have risen in revolt long ago." [22]

The Constitution is not just a collection of noble ideals; it is a practical plan for what works best in a democracy. When we act against the Constitution, our democracy withers. Here's the proof: as professor of international relations Bruce Russett says, democracies "more often win their wars—80 percent of the time." The reason is that "they are more prudent about what wars they get into, choosing wars that they are more likely to win and that will incur lower costs." [23] Of course, we now go to war the way autocracies and dictatorships do: a cowardly press, a somnambulant citizenry, and a violated Constitution make that possible.

Result: we now have a losing streak going, three lost wars in a row. There is no way the quagmire debacles of Vietnam, Iraq, and Afghanistan can be described as victories. These are wars where "winning" cannot even be defined.

3. Right intention

This test may sound bland, but, like the others, it has a bite in it. This test focuses on why you go to war and how you behave when you get there, traditionally called the *jus ad bellum* and *jus in bello*. Right intention warns against blind "support our troops" sloganeering without asking what the troops are being sent to do and how they are doing it. The reasons alleged for the war should be the real reasons for the war.

(a) Undue secrecy and propaganda violate "right intention."
    Secrecy in war, though allegedly for "national security,"
    is often rooted in simple fear of the *vox populi*. (The
    enemy usually knows the secrets.) Secrecy tends to be a
    cover for lies. Propaganda is intrinsically undemocratic
    since it disempowers citizens.

(b) Right intention means that you don't impose unrealistic
    conditions like "unconditional surrender," a demand that
    needlessly postponed the end of World War II. A simi-
    larly nonsensical demand in Iraq is the war will go on
    until there is a flourishing and edifying democracy in
    place. If there were a real democracy there, we would be
    voted out in the morning. Real democracy in Saudi Ara-
    bia and Kuwait would end our commercial interests in
    those countries.

(c) Right intention means we don't use torture.

(d) Right intention means the burdens of the war are distrib-
    uted fairly. We don't just send the poor to do the fighting
    in the spirit of the wealthy father of James Mellon at the
    time of the Civil War: "A man may be a patriot without
    risking his own life or sacrificing his health. There are
    plenty of lives less valuable."[24] Five-deferment Dick
    Cheney could not have said it better.

(e) Right intention means that if you cannot love your ene-
    mies, you will at least try to understand them. Why were
    the 9/11 attackers so highly motivated? Why are 700,000
    Palestinians forced from their homes to make room for
    Israel resentful? Fair questions. If unasked and unan-
    swered, intention is not right.

(f) Intention is not right if those closest to the action are denied the right to conscientious objection. The idea of the soldier as automaton, with no more conscience than a fired bullet, is the keystone of military culture. Blind obedience is as immoral as slavery and if you require it, your intention is not right.

4. The principle of noncombatant immunity

This condition makes a just modern war almost unimaginable. As Archbishop Desmond Tutu says, "In the wars of the 1990s, civilian deaths constituted between 75 and 90 percent of all war deaths. . . . Some two million children have died in dozens of wars during the past decade. . . . This is more than three times the number of battlefield deaths of American soldiers in all their wars since 1776."[25] Our species has not yet evolved morally to the point where it could make this a bedrock principle: what is good for kids is good; what is bad for kids is ungodly. If that principle were accepted, we would find alternatives to war.

If you do something that you know will kill civilians ("shock and awe," atomic bombings of Hiroshima and Nagasaki) in order to get what you want from their government, you are a terrorist. Direct killing of the innocent to make their governments do what you want is terrorism. "Collateral damage" and the old Catholic "principle of double effect" are enlisted to show that we have no responsibility for the "regrettable" by-products of our bombing.[26] ("Sorry, kids, we were after that factory!") You cannot drop uncontrollable bombs on civilians and pretend you don't intend to kill them. However, as modern war developed, this kind of terrorism became standard operating procedure starting in World War II and continuing, with stark irony, in the "war on terror."

Even before modern times, the idea of noncombatant immunity was strained to the point of absurdity. In ancient India, laws were made in a futile effort to spare the "innocent." War was not to visit harm on "those who look on without taking part, those afflicted with grief, those who are asleep, thirsty, or fatigued or are walking along the road, or have a task on hand unfinished, or who are proficient in fine art."[27] The Talmud saw the problem with sieges where warriors and children are lumped together. It ruled that for a siege to be moral, it must not be four-sided but must leave one side open for the innocent to escape. Of course, a three-sided siege with an escape hatch is not a siege. Logic suffers in war. It crumbles before "military necessity."

5. Last resort

The "last resort" principle is simple: resorting to violence when there are neglected alternatives is barbaric. If state-sponsored violence is not our very last resort, we share the same moral ground with hoodlums who solve problems by murder.

6. The Principle of Proportionality

The Principle of Proportionality is the capstone of the JWT. It means that the violence of war must do more good than harm. Nothing wild about that statement. Anything we do should achieve more good than harm. As weapons grow, wars are less and less able to pass this rudimentary test. Wars start their killing even before the first shot is fired, since the preparation for war bankrupts nations and starves the poor.

Since war makers pull out parts of the JWT to hallow their wars, it serves peace well to remind them that their wars have failing moral grades. As Catholic ethicist Joseph Fahey says, "The 'just war' model was never meant to justify war. It was meant to limit war, to control war, and even to avoid war."[28] The allegedly "justified" war is usually the mask of an unconscionable failure to do the advance work of peace and to hide the total embarrassment of statecraft that state-sponsored violence tends to be.

An honest and "strict constructionist" use of the just-war theory challenges the conscience of war makers. Warriors are champions at self-justification. It is patriotic to challenge them. We have to issue a loud *j'accuse* to people like the U.S. Conference of Catholic Bishops, who sanctimoniously and carefully elaborated the principles of JWT in their 1983 pastoral letter, "The Challenge of Peace." Yet, when the United States launches into wars that violate these principles egregiously, the Catholic bishops are bleating about their pelvic obsessions, abortion and same-sex marriage, while the American war crimes proceed. We have to call politicians and "people of faith" before the bar of their professed ideals and charge them with hypocrisy when the charge is merited. It's one of the few tools we have when lying rules the public square and flag-flying "people of faith" prostitute their peacemaking traditions.

But not all "people of faith" are amnesiacs. The Catholic protestor Cindy Sheehan, the Catholic priests Dan and Phil Berrigan, groups like Pax Christi, Call to Action, Voice of the Faithful, joining with all the peacemaking Protestants, Jews, and Muslims, are tapping their religious roots and bringing the ancient protest against collective violence into the present tense. These war critics and peacemakers are not freaks in their traditions. They simply have more retentive memories. They are unmasking the fraudulent claim of the "Christian" religious right that war is the sacramental prelude to the triumph of the "kingdom of God." They are resurrecting the ancient discovery that war is a self-defeating sacrilege. And there is empowering hope in that recovery.

Professor Andrew Bacevich would seem an unlikely soul mate of Cindy Sheehan and the Berrigans. He is a graduate of West Point and a Vietnam veteran. This self-identified "Catholic author," in his stirring book *The New American Militarism: How Americans Are Seduced by War*, is another illustration of how normal it is to be religious and antiwar, to be Catholic and antiwar. He draws inspiration from the Catholic bishops' 1983 pastoral letter on war and peace, which, he notes, "had influence extending far beyond Catholic circles." He unites his hard-nosed empirical analysis of war madness with Pope John XXIII's declaration that "it no longer makes sense to maintain that war is a fit instrument with which to repair the violation of justice."[29]

The Catholic hierarchy are often the last to rouse them-

selves and smell the coffee. But they are stirring, and there is
hope in that. The Pontifical Council for Interreligious Dia-
logue in 2003 offered this understanding of peacemaking:
"Opting for peace does not mean a passive acquiescence in
evil or a compromising of principle. It demands an active
struggle against hatred, oppression, and disunity, but not by
using methods of violence." If those Vatican sentiments
could make it to the pulpits and the pews, a new civic force
for peace could be born.

THE WISDOM OF TEARS

I was amazed, as a young Catholic boy, when I saw on the
back of a Catholic prayer book, the *Missale Romanum*, a
prayer begging for the gift of tears. It said, "Oh God, strike
into the duritiam, the hardness of my heart, and bring forth a
saving flood of tears." As a little boy, I thought, "Who wants
tears? When you grow up you don't have them anymore, especially if you are a man." And that precisely is the problem.
If you are without tears in a world of sorrows, it is a tragedy.
You are not human. And take note, Christians, you are not
Christic. Jesus wept. He looked at that city and said, "If only
you knew the things that make for your peace, but you don't."
And he broke down sobbing. He was like the prophet Jeremiah, who said that unless our eyes run with tears, we will
come to a fearful ruin.

Let us update that Jesus text. Let us have him say,
"America, America, if only you knew the things that make for
your peace, if only you could see that the answer is not in

your weaponry. If only I could, like a mother hen, wrap the wings of my vision around you, wings of justice and peace and compassion, if you could use your great talent and wealth to work to end world hunger, world thirst, world illiteracy, no one would hate you, no one would crash planes into your buildings. You could then burn those war chariots in a holy fire and you would at last know the nourishing energy of peace."

5

Upwardly Mobile Poverty:
An Unnecessary Metastasis

Cartoonists are often the best economists. They're certainly fun. Take, for example, the cartoon that pictured a middle-class family seated around the kitchen table—father, mother, and three children. On the table are bills and a checkbook. The father says, "I've called you all together to let you know that because of inflation, I'm going to have to let two of you go."

Healthy families, of course, do not respond to economic pressures by lopping off heads. There is a bond, a human relationship that prevents that. Where there is human bonding, the sharing of pain is the natural norm.

Inhumane societies do not share pain: they practice human sacrifice. The result is wealth for some, poverty for many.

That's the American story, but with a twist, the "middle class" twist.

"We the people" never meant all of us. When we first spoke those words grandiloquently, they certainly did not include the slaves, the Indians, poor white servants, or voteless women. The special American twist was *the middle-class buffer*: "This became the characteristic of the new nation: finding itself possessed of enormous wealth, it could create the richest ruling class in history, and still have enough for the middle classes to act as a buffer between the rich and the dispossessed."[1] As Richard Hofstader says, we were from the start a middle-class society ruled by the upper classes. The Founding Fathers were not peasants and not without highly vested personal interests in getting England's hand out of their till. George Washington was the richest man in America. John Hancock was a wealthy Boston businessman. Benjamin Franklin was a well-off printer.[2] In modern parlance, the great American revolution was engineered by fat cats with the interests of fat cats very prominently in mind.

It was an uneasy arrangement. At times it required martial law and armed forces to keep the deal they had cooked intact. From slaves, indentured servants, and industrial slaves there were ructions and uprisings, and yet it has to be said, it was overall a stunning long-term success, providing for the highs and the middles a safe distance from the wails of the dispossessed. "This land is my land, but not really your land" was the anthem America sang, and it got away with it for a long time. But now, alas, the lusty joy ride is ending.

THE GREAT UNRAVELING

Poverty is more than a shortage of cash. It doesn't stop with your pocket; it targets your soul. Poverty is a lack of the big interlocking trinity of essential needs: *respect, hope,* and *power*. You can do without anything else, but not these three.

This claim may seem wildly overstated. After all, there are so many things we can't do without: food, water, shelter, a job. All those needs and others collapse into respect, hope, and power. If you do not have food, water, shelter, or a job, you cannot feel respected or hopeful, and you are radically disempowered.

The opposite of respect is insult, and as Aristotle said, insult is the root of all rebellion. In a context of respect, we can endure almost anything. Respect is a recognition that humanity is a shared glory and no one is cutting you out of it. When there is no respect, the slightest snub is galling and unbearable.

There was a fierce interracial fight at Camp Lejeune some years ago. Afterward, officers tried to sort out the causes of this explosion. My brother was a marine officer, and he was assigned to speak with some of the African Americans to try to get to the root of their explosive anger. He heard things that to white ears might sound trivial. For example, at the base store, change was put directly into white hands but put on the counter when a black hand reached out. A black marine being decorated for bravery along with five white companions noticed that the general pinning on the medals paused a bit longer with the white marines and seemed more at home. Neurotic? No. If your flesh is too repulsive for contact, *you* are repulsive. If a white general is not comfortable decorating a hero who saved white lives in battle, how can you ever escape the searing, stigmatizing wounds of racism? We need respect like we need oxygen, and rage erupts when it is missing. That's why poverty is a tinderbox.

If the opposite of respect is insult, the opposite of hope is paralysis. Even old Sisyphus had to be hoping for something or he would have left that stone where he found it and gone fishing, and he would not have gone fishing unless he had hopes for a catch.

Stripped of respect and hope, the fuels of personal power, you are disabled. One of the recent victims of downsizing writes, "One hundred resumes sent in the last six months. No job. Have actually been unemployed for two years. Moved to a new state to start over, about to roll over a cliff. To add to my woes I now doubt my ability to hold a job should I ever get one. I feel like I'm eroding. Once I was extremely adept, flexible, pro-active, etc., etc. Now I feel like sludge." [3]

Those of us who avoided the devastation of poverty are stupid about it. And since our unearned privileges have depended on a poverty slave base, we're defensive and prefer avoiding the subject. But this is a new time. Poverty is on the move from urbia to suburbia. The supports of middle-class security are crumbling like the levees of New Orleans—an economic Katrina, really, with middle-class hopes washing away in a global tide that has hit our shores. Globalization means that American job security is linked with that of all the workers in the world, since corporations with global reach can cherry-pick from anywhere. As yet, international worker alliances are almost nonexistent.

The big squeeze is well on as pensions disappear and health-care benefits shrink while health-care costs balloon. Also slipping: the prospect of getting what was once called fondly "a steady job." (One CEO put it bluntly: "Job security is totally a thing of the past.")[4] On top of that, leisure, and hopes for a lot more of it in retirement, is becoming an upper-upper-class gated monopoly. What's worse, the United States is an empire in decline, and the mood is mean.

Economist Jeff Faux gives a formula for a thirty-year economic binge: first of all, go out and win a world war, leave all potential competitors hobbled, make almost all the world's cars, generate most of its electricity, sit on the world's securest financial institutions, and what do you have? USA post–World War II. But that sweet party time of three-martini lunches peaked in the early 1970s. The national debt rose. Competitors came, saw, and conquered. The erstwhile revelers are now living on borrowed money and borrowed time as the humbled dollar bows before currencies that didn't even exist during that sweet halcyon interval.

During the decline, the economy has been blowing bubbles, first in stocks, then in housing. Now people find themselves "stuck paying off a mountain of debt on homes that are suddenly worth less than the mortgages. They will not only need to keep working: they might also be filing for bankruptcy."[5]

Through all of this the bumbling government outdoes

Nero in irrelevance by fiddling moralistic tunes about same-sex marriages and spending $2 billion a week to wreck Iraq—"fighting terrorism" by stoking more of it. Brilliant!

THE STIGMA COMES HOME

Capitalism from its start had poverty in its train. Serfs in the feudal precapitalist system often had a kind of paternalistic social security. They were part of a unit that shared some essentials out of practical necessity. With the dawn of modern capitalism, the serfs were cast out to scramble for work and security.

Capitalism had two choices from the start: either to correct its deficiencies and care for those who were cast out by the blind mechanisms of the market, or to embark on the systematic vilification of the poor, implying that their plight was their own doing and not an indictment of the system. Capitalism wrapped its arms around that second alternative. Operation Stigmatize had begun.

The Statute of Laborers in 1349 in England made it a crime to give alms to the poor. The Poor Law Reform Bill in England in 1834 said explicitly that the main cause of poverty was the indiscriminate giving of aid, which destroyed the desire to work. Prime Minister Benjamin Disraeli would later say: "It made it a crime to be poor."

In the United States in the nineteenth century, the hugely popular writer Herbert Spencer said that poverty was the direct consequence of sloth and sinfulness. Another writer said, "Next to alcohol, and perhaps alongside it, the most pernicious fluid is indiscriminate soup." Preacher Cotton Mather added religious muscle: "For those who indulge themselves in idleness, the express command of God unto us is that we should let them starve."[6]

There developed what could be called the sacramentality of wealth. The doctrine of "predestination" rode to the rescue of the privileged. It was God who divided humanity up into the saved and the damned. Wealth came to be seen as a sign of God's favor, and then, in a double whammy, poverty came to be seen as a mark of God's disgust. Bishop Lawrence of Massachusetts intoned: "In the long run, it is only to the man of morality that wealth comes. . . . Godliness is in league with riches."[7] (Bishops ought to talk more and intone less.)

Pouring salt on the wounds of stigma is politically useful. Ronald Reagan slandered poor women with his "welfare queens" insult, and Governor Kirk Fordice told reporters in Mississippi that all that the poor needed was a "good alarm clock."[8] Senator Russell Long insisted that the welfare system was being "abused by malingerers, cheaters, and outright frauds."[9] Poor women are especially demeaned. Putting a "family cap" on welfare assistance is based on the false assumption that women are mindless copulators, reproducing irresponsibly. In fact, since 1975 the average welfare family has two children, the same as the national average . . . and that in spite of efforts to deprive poor women of contraceptives and abortion rights.[10]

The poor are lazy—that is capitalist dogma. In return for a paltry welfare check they must be forced to work. This, Michael Harrington said, is the modern version of the workhouse. He sees it first in full bloom in Newburgh, New York, in 1961, where the city fathers decreed that those on the dole must work for their payments. "This sub-minimum wage and non-union employment would, it was thought, inculcate the Protestant ethic."[11] We're still at it. The Personal Responsibility and Work Opportunity Reconciliation Act of 1996 mandated that recipients of public assistance work in return for their checks.

One victim who had gotten accepted into Hunter College in New York City was told she would have to work thirty hours a week or her family would lose their support. "They offered me jobs working in the park, cleaning toilets, cleaning transportation."[12] There goes college! "New York City has one of the most sophisticated systems of higher education in the country, but welfare recipients are essentially shut out of it," says Wendy Bach, an attorney in the Urban Justice Center who works with welfare recipients.[13] This, of course, assures that our slave base does not get uppity, sporting college degrees and stuff like that. (President George W. Bush agreed with this policy, saying that college is not really work and it does not teach "the importance of work." His own personal record would seem to support that view.)

But now, the stigma of poverty has moved from the downstairs to the upstairs people, including those with college degrees. The *college = affluence* myth is evanescing for many of the downwardly mobile members of the middle class, victims of layoffs, downsizings, and outsourcings who, all of a sudden, moved from marketer to janitor. "They shrink off in shame—after all, they must have done something wrong—and vanish from the unemployment statistics by going to Circuit City or Starbucks." [14] The poverty stigma has migrated up.

Of course, the "lazy drones" theory of poverty is a big lie. The inconvenient truth, as a Brookings Institution study put it, is this: "Poor people—males and females, blacks and whites, youths and adults—identify their self-esteem with work as strongly as do the non-poor. They express as much willingness to take job training if unable to earn a living. . . . They have, moreover, as high life aspirations as do the non-poor and want the same things, among them a good education and a nice place to live. . . . [There are] no differences between poor and non-poor when it comes to life goals and wanting to work." [15]

THE NEOLIBERAL SUCKING SOUND

"Neoliberal" is a weird misnomer since this theory is not new or liberal. It could be better labeled "right-wing, ultraconservative greed" theory. It's the mother's milk of neoconservatism. It rests on a self-serving faith in the unfettered market as a savior that should be allowed to make the major decisions for a society and for the world.

Government is the problem, not the solution, as Ronald Reagan preached. (It truly was the problem during his tenure as president.) He curbed trade unions and freed corporations. Neoliberals think workers and other citizens should get less social protection and instead should await the blessings that will trickle down from corporate heaven. Competition is the Darwinian law of life, and, of course, in competition, as in any sporting event, some win and some lose. Neoliberalism is the spoiled, bratty child of the winners.

The unmentionable goal of all of this is the transfer of wealth from the bottom to the top, and it really works. Maggie Thatcher, a true believer, made it work. In pre-Thatcher Britain, about one in ten persons were classed as living below the poverty line. When she left, one in four and one child in three were officially poor. In Reagan's reign, the bottom 80 percent lost something while top earners flourished.[16] The genius of the rich beneficiaries of this system is that they have convinced the deprived to vote for their own impoverishment. Look at the length of Thatcher's tenure and the long Republican hegemony in the United States. Somehow the ripped-off bought the TINA lie—TINA: *There Is No Alternative*. Actually, the truth is TAOA: *There Are Other Alternatives, oodles of them!*

Comparisons are not always odious; they are often tough teachers. U.S. capitalism is not the only model. Let's travel a bit. First stop, Sweden. Take note: Sweden lives in a hot spot, having had neighbors such as Nazi Germany and the Soviet Union. The country has not been at war in two hundred years, which already tells us they're not like us. Their capitalism is not like ours either. Swedes are entitled to eighteen months of paid maternity leave with job protection that can be prorated over the first eight years of a child's life. How's that for "family values"? We're not like that.

Next, let's visit France, the best friend the United States ever had. First they helped free us from the clutches of the

British Empire; next they warned us not to waste blood and fortune in Vietnam. They gave a similar warning on Iraq. (Out of simple gratitude we should drink French wine and do a lot of French kissing. It's the least we could do.) France provides universal child care to all toilet-trained children, and single mothers receive government payments until their children are over the age of three.[17] (In a recent priority-revealing study, the U.S. median wage of child-care workers was three cents an hour less than that of parking lot attendants!)[18] A United Nations study reported that the United States is one of only six countries that does not have a policy requiring paid maternity leave.[19]

Misopedia. Now there's an ugly word. It's ugly because it is an unnecessary and euphemizing use of Greek. It means the hatred of children, just as the word misogyny means the hatred of women. Greeking those words softens the blow. I take it as an incontrovertible axiom of morality that *what is good for kids is good and what is bad for kids is ungodly.* I should say *almost* incontrovertible, since once, in giving a talk to a large and politically diverse group, I opened with that "good for kids" principle as something that right and left could agree on. One person disagreed, a low-level member of the Reagan administration whose name repulsion has helped me forget. He feared that such a principle could subvert some essential economic dogmas. And right he was, given the dogmas that are deemed essential in neoliberalism. Kids are front-line casualties when safety nets are shredded and when kill-power trumps spending for life.

Neoliberalism treats workers like it treats children.

Again, there are gentler models of capitalism. In Germany, companies with over three hundred workers are required by law to give workers seats on their supervisory boards. Medium-sized and large companies must also have workers' councils with a determinative voice on downsizings, compensation packages, and job security.[20] "Europeans' longer vacation times, four to six weeks, are protected by legislation. The higher productivity rate of the United States is tied to more hours, not to greater productivity per worker per hour."[21] American workers work on average almost nine full weeks more per year than most European workers, according to the International Labor Organization, a United Nations agency.[22] This is all part of the leisure famine neoliberalism plans for the underclass. "The idle mind," after all, "is the devil's workshop."

Neoliberals love "voluntary" solutions to problems. This is the "trust us" nostrum that never works. As economist Theodore Levitt observes: "Organized business has been chronically hostile to every humane and popular reform in the history of American capitalism."[23] The moral spirit of business shows in the salaries of the new royalty, now called CEOs. The CEO of ExxonMobil makes $13,700 an hour, while the CEO of Wal-Mart has to eke along at $3,500 per hour. Meanwhile, the full-time minimum-wage worker earns $10,000 a year.[24] When I have asked businesspeople about the high salaries of executives, I am told that this is "incentive" pay. The obvious question is: if it takes $13,000 an hour to give you an incentive to do your job, why not find work you are more interested in? These royals allege "trickle-down," but they practice "gush-up." To tame their gorging, what is needed is a maximum-wage bill. Oh, the howls from the well-heeled that suggestion would evoke!!

SOLUTIONS: ARE THE POOR BETTER OFF THAN THEY WERE FOUR YEARS AGO?

Amazingly, there are antidotes to the savagery of neoliberal neocons buried in the hidden treasure stores of the American theocracy. Supreme Court justice David Brewer was not a loner at the end of the nineteenth century when he said, "This is a Christian nation."[25] There are a lot of David Brewers still among us, as we saw when the George W. Bush administration turned them loose. The radical right has effectively hijacked the Bible, but they know not what they clutch to their bosom. Scholarship can easily hoist them on their biblical petard. In fact, good biblical scholarship is a civil service in this land of ours. A little Bible sophistication is essential equipment for informed U.S. citizens. Secular as many citizens may be, they are being Bible-whacked by right-wing distortions of biblical politics. Ignoring that fact would be like reformers in Iran ignoring Islam.

Right-wing Jesus people should be invited to meet the real guy.

Rabbi Jesus would never have made it as an editorial writer for the *Wall Street Journal*. Their gospel is "good news to the rich." Jesus, a bona fide left-winger, said that his mission was "good news to the poor" (Luke 4:18). He was a true Jew in this: "Open wide your hand to the poor and the distressed" (Deut. 15:11). The ancients believed, as Tacitus tells us, that the gods are with the mighty. The Israelite morality in which Jesus was reared dissented. The Jewish tradition began to image the divine differently—and remember, God talk always shows where your moral heart is. After some high and mighty and bellicose God talk, the ancient Hebrews switched and presented their God as "a God of the humble . . . the poor . . . the weak . . . the desperate . . . and the hopeless"—not exactly the types you find on the floor of an American political convention (Judg. 9:11).

Quite simply, the goal of biblical morality is the total elimination of poverty: "There shall be no poor among you!" (Deut. 15:4), because "the poverty of the poor is their ruin" (Prov. 10:15). And the Bible doesn't purvey spacey idealism. Its ideals have bottom-line practicality. In contrast to biblical economics, it is stunning to see the frivolous things that win Nobel prizes in economics. The Nobel Committee should redeem itself by awarding a posthumous prize to Isaiah for these seven words alone: "The effect of justice will be peace" (Isa. 32:17). Peace is the payload of justice. If you plant justice, you reap peace. Only when justice is established will people "live in a tranquil country" with all their cities "peaceful" and their "homes full of ease" (Isa. 32:19). No other scheme—political, economic, or military—will achieve this effect. You may, like the United States, have military installations all around the world and pour more than $400 billion a year into enough weaponry to destroy all human life dozens of times over, but "the effect" will not be peace. You may, like modern Israel, store up hundreds of atomic weapons and have one of the strongest military forces in the world, but "the effect" will not be peace. Kill-power doesn't deliver. Justice does.

Biblical justice shifts the burden of poverty from the poor to the rich. The assumption is that the well-off have cooked the deals that have made them fat. So, quite logically, the Bible says, put the burden where the power is. The term "rich" in the Bible does not refer to only a Bill Gates or a Warren Buffett. It means "economically secure." If you know today that, if you're alive one year from now, you will be sure of having breakfast, lunch, and supper, you are in Bible terms "rich," and the Bible considers you guilty until proven innocent. "Woe to you rich," said Jesus (Luke 6:20–24). The assumption was that security chills the conscience. In a bit of rhetorical overkill, Jesus said that getting the comfortable to identify with the needs of the poor is like getting a camel through the eye of a needle (Mark 10:25–27).

Jeremiah blasts those who "grow rich and grand, bloated and rancorous, their thoughts are all of evil and they refuse to do justice to the orphan and to the poor"(Jer. 5:25–28). The rich are accused of "building Zion in bloodshed" (Mic. 3:10). "The spoils of the poor are in your houses" (Isa. 3:14). Amos accused the rich of using the blood of the poor to mix the mortar that held up their palaces.

The cure is simple but distasteful to the polysaturated. The cure is appropriate modes of redistribution. "Bread is life to the destitute, and it is murder to deprive them of it" (Eccles. 34:21). Proactive redistribution: if people are weak, it is your problem to find them and make them strong (Lev.

25:35), because the well-off folks are implicated in their
weakness. In the biblical view, "most privilege is not earned,
and most poverty is not deserved. . . . People largely get their
poverty or their wealth depending on their location in the
class system."[26]

Jesus, of course, was the product of a Jewish mother. We
don't know whether she gave him chicken soup when he had
a cold, but we do know that she gave him a conscience. After
all, two of her sons, Jesus and James, were killed as rebels, so
she had to have been special. And, of course, she gave that
short speech while rejoicing in God. The God she rejoices in
wants to fill the hungry "with good things" and strip the rich
of their ill-gotten gains. The "arrogant of heart" and the
"monarchs" are to be routed and the "humble" are to be
lifted high (Luke 1:46–55).

The bottom line of all this: nothing else works. Make the
interests of the poor your interests or society corrodes and
you will have to hide from the effects of the corrosion in
gated communities with big locks and nervous alarm systems. A nation of benighted housing projects and gated communities cannot endure. Wealth built on a poverty base is a
house "built on sand"(Matt. 7:26).

"Are the poor better off than they were four years ago?"
That's the Bible's question to any society.

The George W. Bush White House had Bible-study
sessions that were de rigeur. What in the world were they
studying?[27]

THE LEFT-WING CORE OF CATHOLICISM

Just as it is a big lie that all Catholics are antichoice on abortion, it is another big lie that Catholics are mainly right-wing greedomaniacs. And we're not just talking Catholic left-wing academics who care about ending poverty. We're talking popes and saints and core Catholic teachings and traditional Catholic folks. If the Democratic Party could break free of the chains of lobbyocracy, it would again find Catholics as their natural constituents. As my Irish uncles used to say, when they came to America they looked for three things right off: the nearest Catholic Church, the nearest pub, and the headquarters of the Democratic Party.

There is something old-time Catholic about joining a political party. If you want to get something done, first clarify your ideas and then get friends—i.e., socialize your idea; group power moves history, not personal piety. That's why Catholic workers also took to unions right off.

In the Reagan-Bush years, "Catholic involvement in politics has largely been hijacked by a small but committed group of lay and clerical activists who represent the rightist fringe of the political and economic spectrum, not the views of a majority of American Catholics." That is the conclusion of a study by University of Alabama professor Glenn Feldman.[28] He continues, "Catholic right-wing extremists" have bypassed "traditional Catholic doctrine on war, poverty, economics, and social concerns" and successfully, for a time, tied "the faith, and its considerable numbers and resources, to the fortunes of the modern-day Republican Party." This was helped along by the "negligence, torpor, and timidity of the bulk of America's Catholic hierarchy." I would add that it was much helped by my American colleagues in Catholic theology, most of whom sat on their hands as this hijacking progressed.

The preferential option for the poor. That phrase became the mantra for modern Catholic economics. As Catholic ethicist Barbara Andolsen puts it: "Roman Catholic social thought does not adopt an impartial standpoint; it adopts a moral stance of advocacy for the socially disadvantaged and the economically vulnerable."[29] In this it mirrors the biblical passion for the *anawim*, the Hebrew word for the exploited and left-out poor, the have-nots who are being had by the powerful haves and by the deals that the powerful have set up to keep wealth gushing to the top.

On this "option for the poor," popes and bishops led the charge. As nineteenth-century industrialism boomed, Pope Leo XIII, though in many ways a social conservative and phobic about "socialists," saw that the emerging forms of capitalism were leaving the working class with "a yoke little better than slavery itself."[30] He conceded that governments had obligations to both rich and poor, but he insisted: "When it comes to protecting the rights of individuals, the poor and the helpless have a claim to special consideration."[31] Leo saw that "freedom" in the economic sphere is often a mask for exploitation. He saw desperate workers accepting harsh and dangerous work while employers called it "voluntary bargaining." Leo blew off the fluff of freedom talk and saw those workers as "the victims of force and injustice." [32] If you are so subdued that you don't resist the overwhelming power of the rapist, you are still raped.

Pope-loving right-wingers and sweatshop defenders ("they would be worse off if we weren't here") should hear this pope: "Rich men and masters should remember this— that to exercise pressure for the sake of gain, upon [the economically vulnerable], and to make one's profit out of the need of another, is condemned by all laws, human and divine. To defraud any one of wages that are his due is a crime that cries out to the avenging anger of heaven." [33]

Pope John Paul II was no raving liberal (he never met a contraceptive he didn't hate), but the Catholic social justice tradition resonated in his teaching. Solidarity with workers and the poor was the only way to be faithful to the witness of Jesus, he insisted. That witness calls us to be "the church of the poor." [34] "The church of the poor"—and that's the pope speaking.

Ownership in the Catholic tradition is not an absolute. Pope John Paul insisted that owning is never divorced from owing. In his choice metaphor, there is a "social mortgage" on all private property. [35] Ownership of the means of production is illegitimate if the rights of the workers to fair wages and safe working conditions are trashed. The owners, in a word, have to "serve labor." [36] Protecting the human rights of workers can hurt the deep-pocket people. Pope Paul VI had a message that would well serve platform-drafting committees of the political parties: "The Gospel instructs us in the preferential respect due to the poor and the special situation they have in society: the more fortunate should renounce some of their rights so as to place their goods more generously at the service of others."[37]

The United States Conference of Catholic Bishops has said that this left-wing social thinking is rock solid in the biblical and Catholic tradition and is a summons to the consciences of all who call themselves Catholic. It is "at the heart of the Church . . . integral to the proclamation of the Gospel and part of the vocation of every Christian today."[38] It is, the bishops insist, as old as the Hebrew prophets and as compelling as the Sermon on the Mount. This summons disqualifies Catholics as members of "the Christian Right" or "the Christian Coalition."

I cite bishops and popes, the most conservative spokespersons of the tradition, to show that even they are deeply rooted in the biblical left-wing passions. Beyond them, plowing the same turf with vigor, there is the Catholic feminist movement, spurred by the entrance for the first time in history of Catholic women theologians. Also, the Catholic theology from Latin America that came to be called "liberation theology" springs from the poor world with a powerful prophetic bite. These have become the goads and teachers of "First World" Catholic thinkers to good effect.

If Catholic preachers could get off the pelvic issues and get back to the heart of the Catholic social justice tradition, Catholics could, if cured from the fevers of affluenza, once again become part of the solution.

REENFRANCHISING COMMON SENSE

Anything that can be solved by money is not a problem . . . *if* the money is there. The money *is* there to solve the poverty problem, nationally and internationally. Some 40 million people die every year from hunger and poverty-related causes—the equivalent of three hundred jumbo-jet crashes daily—with half of the passengers being children.[39] That could be solved by money. If a glass of pure water would cure AIDS, many people in the world would have no access to it. The money to solve all that and more is there, but money galore is being squandered in absurd ways, and the father of all misspent money is military spending, the idol that the United States and most nations of the world worship.

Let's take a little journey into madness. Let's visit the USS *Kitty Hawk*. This ship is like a nuclear-powered floating city. It is almost three football fields long, as tall as a twenty-story building, and it houses over five thousand crew, pilots, and mechanics as well as seventy sleek and lethal aircraft. It is never lonely; keeping it company are a mighty Aegis cruiser, frigates and destroyers, two hunter-killer submarines, as well as supply vessels.

Impressive? Yes, but embarrassing. "The United States has thirteen of these carrier battle groups. No other country has even one."[40] It's a bit like having the best football team in the world and no opponents. And this is just one example of military waste in the great big bloated offense budget.

The U.S. economy has come to spend more than $30

million per hour—over ten thousand dollars per second—on its military. Even the collapse of Soviet communism, the designated enemy, did not stay this wasteful profusion. An undefined "terrorism" has taken its place as the *bête du jour*.[41]

Putting aside my own view that 10 percent of the United States military budget would be adequate for all our reasonable military purposes, I submit more conservative figures. Long before the collapse of communism in the Soviet Union and Eastern Europe, the Center for Defense Information (staffed by retired military officers) estimated that one-third of our expenditures served no military purpose. Some even estimated that one-half of the budget would provide for all imaginable military needs. Since the collapse of communism, others have joined in even lower estimates. Thus, it is conservative to say that at least $10 million per hour (of the more than $30 million per hour now spent) could be diverted to nonmilitary purposes. Starting with the first $1 million, here are some possibilities to stoke our moral-political imagination.

THE FIRST MILLION

With the first $1 million per hour, coming to $24 million a day, we transform American education. Through history we have honored the teachers of our children and starved them. We could end that shame by immediately doubling the salaries of K–12 teachers . . . on the wild assumption that they are worth at least as much as lawyers. By removing this money from military misuse we can remove school aid from inequitable and inconsistent property tax schemes. We could institute fully paid sabbaticals for K–12 teachers to let them keep up with the latest developments in their field, thus allowing, in some cases, for major retooling.

We could put some of our idle explosives to good use by combining them and many bulldozers to raze every inferior school structure in the nation—putting in their place buildings full of light, beauty, practicality, and hope. (We could allow the child who writes the best essay to push down the dynamite trigger plunger that razes the old school!) We cut the teacher-student ratio and lower it further for students with special language or other needs. Some of our liberated monies will flow to the universities, since our need for teachers will at least double. The genius now present in our overworked teachers will be allowed to explode as they themselves decide how to improve teaching. Prematurely retired people who have forgotten that financial security without fulfillment can lead to death by boredom could be lured back into part-time teaching.

Increasingly the lower economic classes are being priced out of college education. Why not heed Adolph Reed's suggestion of "a GI bill for everybody"? Under the GI Bill, World War II veterans usually received full tuition support and generous stipends (up to $12,000 in 1994 dollars). A 1988 report by a congressional subcommittee on education and health estimated that 40 percent of those who attended college would not otherwise have done so without aid. The report also found that each dollar spent educating that 40 percent produced a $6.90 return due to increased national output and increased federal tax revenues resulting from the more educated citizenry. For less than $50 billion a year (the cost of six months of fighting the second Gulf War), all public college and university tuition could be free for all qualified students.

The economic and security gains from all of this? A highly skilled workforce. There would be alternatives to despair in our poverty zones. Lower unemployment would follow as buildings are constructed and equipped, and new teachers get hired. We could anticipate technological advances from better-educated researchers. When it comes to creativity, "fortune favors the prepared mind."

THE SECOND MILLION

With the next $1 million per hour, we could seed the private sector to find new energy sources, creating more jobs at the same time. The first goal of this industry would be to put solar paneling on every suitable roof in this country in X number of years. The supply of oil is finite, and therefore environmentally benign substitutes are necessary. Generous grants, free training programs, and low-interest loans could be made available to aspiring entrepreneurs. Scholarships for technical schools and funds for research universities would be made available. We could begin to catch up in the search for new forms of energy. In April 1988 a Soviet passenger plane, the TU 155 (comparable in size to the Boeing 727), took off from a Moscow airport on a test flight powered by hydrogen rather than petroleum-based fuel. We did not respond to this event as we did to Sputnik because we believed that, unlike Sputnik, the TU 155 had little military importance. We are more responsive to fear than to hope—current budgets show that. With 71 percent of our federal research monies allotted to military purposes, there has been little left for anything more beneficent.

THE THIRD MILLION

The next $1 million per hour could be directed toward redirecting the work of the many good people who make a living on military contracts. Our purpose is not to put them and the military contractors out of business. We would direct these people toward transportation, first turning bomber makers into train makers. American trains are among the least developed in the world. Press reports advise us that they are frequently off the tracks, and when on the tracks they go nowhere very quickly. Meanwhile, trains in Japan, Germany, and France move at speeds of 180 miles per hour. Japanese scientists have tested the magnetic levitation train at 319 miles per hour. Although the idea for this train was born in the United States, it was shunted aside in favor of weapons research. (Actually, I think that 319 miles an hour is too fast. You could not even see the cows! "Was that a cow?" "No, I think it was Chicago.") We have spent 170 times as much on space travel in recent years as on terrestrial transit. The results are painfully visible in cluttered airports and abandoned rail tracks, and on the 40 percent of our bridges and 60 percent of our roads that have languished in serious disrepair since the beginning of the 1990s.

THE NEXT FEW MILLION

Other problems of health and well-being could be met by redirecting several other military millions. We could eliminate the category of the "uninsured patient" from our healthcare lexicon. The government should become the insurer of last resort, as works well in the other industrial nations of the West. We could consider making all medical schools tuition free, with admission based on talent and commitment alone. In return, new doctors would be required to serve for two or three years in poor, medically deprived areas—something that would give them clinical experience they would not get elsewhere. We could supply the number of drug treatment centers that are actually needed—while not forgetting that the best drug treatment is a job-filled economy. Poverty, despair, and drug abuse often correlate.

Scientists redirected from war to peace could help plan for future major earthquakes in California and elsewhere. Poisoned lakes and groundwaters could be redeemed, topsoil restored, fish sources replenished, and forests saved. The technology is already available to turn deserts into gardens, as illustrated by projects in Israel and elsewhere. The deserts can rejoice, as the biblical poets imagined.

We could address the pressing population crises. Projections show the world's population growing to as many as 8 billion, or even 11 billion, people by 2050, almost all of them in poor nations. Hope and the education of women are the best contraceptives. Health care, access to food, and universal education are the ingredients of hope, and without it people will not plan reasonable birthrates. If decency does not move us regarding the calamities afflicting people who live in the Third World, fear should. For the first time in history the poor can hurt us, because poverty is now as global as finance. While the rich are rapid ecology-wreckers, the poor do it slowly as they denude their land out of desperation, and the poisonous results come home to us in the air, the water, the beef, and the strawberries.

Solving all this is not beyond our fiscal reach, though it seems to beyond our moral grasp. Let's not forget the possible solutions already on the table, like economist James Tobin's Nobel Prize–winner's suggestion of a 0.5 percent tax on all transactions in foreign exchange. The Tobin tax on foreign-exchange transactions would help dampen speculative international financial movements but would be too small to deter commodity trade or serious international investments. The money could be used to retire the unwieldy debts of poor countries, and it could finance the efforts of the United Nations and other agencies and nongovernmental organizations to bring education, soil conservation, water purification, microloans for cottage industries, family planning, AIDS education and prevention, and improved communications throughout the world. All of this could be done for a pittance. It is estimated that basic health care and nutrition for all the world's poor could be had for a mere $15 billion a year, basic education for everyone for what it takes to fight the Iraq war for five weeks, and so on. If the United States took the lead in all of this, it would have nothing to fear from terrorism. As historian Howard Zinn often reminds us, generous and modest nations have nothing to fear from terrorists.

Poverty is not an unsolvable problem. This list gives only a few of the benefits that come when the human spirit is freed of the military stranglehold. The result is peace, in the sense of the Hebrew *shalom*, which means more than just the absence of war. It implies fullness of life and a triumph of human intelligence in a community where needs are met and joy is possible. Peace is the only rational goal of economics or politics. Peace is the absence of poverty. Our current budget is a form of necro-economics with poverty programmed in at its base.

The Hebrew prophets would be shouting at us, "Have you eyes and cannot see; have you ears and cannot hear?" Or in more modern parlance: "What are you, stupid already?"

6

Earth Threats, Earth Hopes

If you have just a wee bit of whimsy left over from your childhood, you would have to admit that it was a really neat idea. Larry Walters always wanted to be a pilot, but his eyesight was weak. Still, the dream did not die. Sitting in his Los Angeles backyard, watching the planes soaring overhead, desire turned the dream into a scheme. Larry would get some helium balloons, attach them to his deck chair, float some one hundred feet above his neighbors, sip a beer or two, and then pop his balloons with his pellet gun and descend slowly for a celebration with friends.

Talk about nothing failing like success!

On July 2, 1982, Larry took off. Did he ever take off! When his friends cut the cords that tied his Sears deck chair to the ground, Larry quickly departed this earth and rose to an altitude of sixteen thousand feet. Airplanes zoomed by him, above him, and below him as he floated toward the Long Beach airport. Stunned commercial pilots reported the shocking news to the control tower. "We have spotted a man flying at sixteen thousand feet on a deck chair!"

After a forty-five-minute flight, Larry began popping balloons until his dangling cables got caught on power lines, causing a blackout in the Long Beach area. As he disembarked uninjured from his aircraft, the Los Angeles Police Department was his humorless welcoming committee. Poor Larry. He was fined $4,000 by the Federal Aviation Administration for operating an aircraft without an "airworthiness certificate." That seems so unfair: imagine how hard it would have been to get that airworthiness certificate even if he had taken his deck chair down to the FAA office. He was also penalized for failing to establish radio contact with nearby control towers. Picky, picky!

Larry told a waiting reporter, "A man can't just sit around."[1]

Larry won top prize that year from the Bonehead Club of Dallas, and that's a shame, since he was a teacher and, indeed, a symbol for our age. What Larry taught is that technology can take you whither you would not go. It has a mind of its own.

Neat ideas that are technically feasible are always chockfull of surprises. Scientific genius and prescience are not joined at the hip.

Ford's Model T's were a neat idea. Mr. Ford agreed with Larry: "A man can't just sit around." Speed, convenience, and no more horse droppings on our roads! We all cheered: Hello, tomorrow, we have a beautiful feeling; everything's going our way!

But, oops! Later came the Larry moment, and we were aloft on an oil economy with no pellet guns to bring us down without injury. Our horseless machines now have their own excrement, and it can't be used for fertilizer. Instead, their detritus goes up as well as down, trapping heat and helping to double-baste the planet in CO_2, melting the polar ice and swelling the seas, and rewriting our geography in the process.

Chemistry and physics, like Larry, could not "just sit around" either. Joined to the medical arts, they extended our lives and gave us comforts and cures the Caesars would envy. But, in another oops! Larry moment, they also gave us more detritus, much of it seeping into our blood and into our genes. Chemistry, like Larry, zoomed. There are more than seventy thousand chemicals in use on our earthly habitat, with hundreds being added each year. Most have not been tested for safety, and it is estimated that as many as half of them are toxic to humans.[2] Human breast milk often contains more toxins than are permissible in milk sold by dairies. And some toxins are so ubiquitous and pervasive that many are permitted by dairies. Human bodies at death often contain enough toxins and metals to be classified as hazardous waste, and male sperm counts worldwide have fallen by 50 percent since 1938. Our chemicals poison and kill whales and dolphins and birds and little fungi.[3]

We are the exterminator species. Some scientists predict that in this century, if current trends continue, we might drive 50 percent of the world's plant and animal species to extinction.[4] (And recall that death is the end of life; extinction is the end of birth.) The planet is now a coal mine with all kinds of canaries dropping. Others compare our wiping out of other species on whom we depend to rivets popping out of the wings of an airplane. How many rivets can a plane lose before it crashes?

Twenty-five percent of the drugs prescribed in the United States are derived from wild organisms.[5] An obscure fungus found in the mountains of Norway produces a powerful suppressor of the human immune system, allowing transplants to take hold.[6] If we are species-ists who feel that nothing in nature matters unless it helps us, we—gross though we be—should be self-serving enough to protect the biodiversity that has been so generous to us! Our dopey species is like a fetus rebelling against the womb that holds it.

Science is a wholly owned subsidiary of the natural environment. We forgot that. We fussed with Mother Nature, and she is mad.

SAPIENS—REALLY?

How is the species that calls itself (somewhat prematurely) *sapiens* responding to this? Mostly with its highly developed art of distraction. Our technical addictions are tyrannical, as all addictions are, and tyrants require distraction to stay in control of the masses. The old Roman satirist Juvenal mocked the Roman people, telling them that all it took for emperors to tyrannize them was to distract them with "bread and circuses, *panem et circenses*."[7] (Pizza and football are some of the modern equivalents.)

That oft-quoted saying of Juvenal is used without noting a brilliant psychological insight he included. He said that the people who gobble up the bread and devour the circuses are nonetheless *anxius*, worried. There's hope in that, because if we're not worried, we're doomed. If we get worried enough,

we may start to fix problems. Worrying today is a civic obliga-
tion. Hey, the oceans are coming! The deserts are expanding!
We need a worried ethic, not armies, to defend against these
threats.

Our talent for avoidance teeters between comedy and
tragedy. As the presidency of George W. Bush was sinking, a
cartoon pictured the president at a press conference. A reporter asks, "Mr. President, Iraq and Afghanistan are in
chaos, polar ice is melting, the dollar is sinking, most of the
world hates us, the national debt is soaring, the middle class is
disappearing; what response do you have to all of that?"
Mr. Bush replied, "Marriage is between a man and a woman."

The history of our species is full of such epics of denial.
Remote little Easter Island is but one cruel example. It lies
two thousand miles off the west coast of South America. It
was once a thriving society of some seven thousand people
who had a penchant for carving massive stone statues—some
twenty feet in height—and then moving them and erecting
them around the island. Lacking any hauling animals, they
used tree trunks as rollers to move these multi-ton feats
around the island. Big problem. By the year 1600 they had
run out of trees, and with that their society collapsed. When
a Dutch ship visited the island in 1722, it found three thousand primitive people living in squalor, engaged in perpetual
warfare and resorting to cannibalism. It is a little island. One
could walk around it in a day or so. People should have noticed that they were running out of trees. They didn't.[8]

Meanwhile, back here today, the Maldive Islands are
itsy-bitsy islands in the Indian Ocean a thousand miles south

of India. A population of 275,000 lives there, where the highest point is five feet above sea level. Not for long, it seems. Now during storms the whole island is underwater. "Come see us while we're still here," their Ministry of Tourism advertises. At the Rio Earth Summit in 1992, Maldive president Maumoon Abdul Gayoom told the president of the United States, George H. W. Bush, that a few feet of ocean rise will be the end of his country. "Not to worry," Bush replied, in unconscious imitation of King Canute. "The United States will not allow that to happen to the Maldives."[9] He then returned home to preside over the pollution event that the United States had become.

The good news, in a hedged sort of way, is that some say it is not too late. Christopher Flavin of Worldwatch Institute (which has led the wise worriers for years) greeted 2007 with a *Worldwatch Magazine* editorial entitled "It May Not Be Too Late." That's about as reassuring as a pilot announcing, "This plane may not crash." Others are not even that sanguine about our ecological plight.

Recently, the ecological pessimists have been the realists. It's wise to give them a hearing. Georg Henrik von Wright says with chilling calmness, "One perspective, which I don't find unrealistic, is of humanity as approaching its extinction as a zoological species. The idea has often disturbed people. . . . For my part I cannot find it especially disturbing. Humanity as a species will at some time with certainty cease to exist; whether it happens after hundreds of thousands of years or after a few centuries is trifling in the cosmic perspective. When one considers how many species humans have made an end of, then such a natural nemesis can perhaps seem justified."[10] Vaclav Havel warns that if we endanger the earth she will dispense with us in the interest of a higher value—that is, life itself. Biologist Lynn Margulis joins the grim chorus, saying that the rest of earth's life did very well without us in the past and it will do very well without us in the future.[11]

New York University physics professor Marty Hoffert adds, "It may be that we're not going to solve global warming, the earth is going to become an ecological disaster, and somebody will visit in a few hundred million years and find there were some intelligent beings who lived here for a while, but they just couldn't handle the transition from being hunter-gatherers to high technology. It's entirely possible."[12]

A dire conclusion presses in on us: *if current trends continue, we will not.*

It is possible—and has been gloomily argued—that the two greatest disasters to hit this generous planet have been (1) the asteroidal pummeling of 65 million years ago that extinguished the dinosaurs et al., and (2) the arrival of the rogue species that calls itself the *animal rationale*—the rational animal.

Actually, these modern Cassandras are no more pessimistic about our self-destructive proclivities than is the Bible. The same Bible that sees us as made "in the image of God"—a metaphor for infinite perfectability—first paints a picture of us as downright hopeless. "The Lord looks down from heaven on all humankind to see if any act wisely. . . . But all are disloyal, all are rotten to the core; no one does anything good, no, not even one" (Ps. 14:2–3). Even our best efforts seem polluted: "our righteous deeds [are] like a filthy rag" (Isa. 64:5–7). "Can the Nubian change his skin, or the leopard its spots? And you, can you do good, you who are schooled in evil?" (Jer. 13:23). All "rotten to the core"! Ouch!

Bible scholar Gerd Theissen piles on more here, noting that we have long been preoccupied with finding the "missing link" between apes and true humanity. Call off the search, he says; we are that missing link. True humanity has not yet arrived in the evolutionary process. True humanity could not be hell-bent on "terracide" and endless slaughter by way of hunger and war, as we thus far have been. As we noted in the last chapter, "About 40 million people die every year from hunger and related diseases—equivalent to 300 jumbo-jet crashes every day—with half of the passengers being children." [13] True humanity?

OUR UNFLATTERING HISTORY

Any species that can go from candlelight to moon exploration to chess-playing computers in a century seems pretty sharp. But wait. This outburst of fancy tools and toys is not typical. In the long-haul view, we look fairly myopic. When I took a stab at golf some years ago, I had the preternatural gift of a decent drive on the first tee. That was a mercy, since that's when waiting golfers are standing around to watch your performance. As I strutted out onto the fairway, they must have thought me a tower of power. That, sad to tell, was the last time I ever saw the fairway. For the rest of the day I thrashed about in the trees and underbrush, my balls seeking out water with the skill of a thirsty gazelle. The message? Take a long-haul view before judging.

In the long haul, humans look dumb. As our intelligence budded and began to bloom over a million years, it wasn't until ten thousand years ago that we discovered that you could plant stuff: the agricultural "Duh" moment. Prior to that, we didn't seem to be able to figure out why orange trees grew up around orange trees and crabgrass grew up around crabgrass. We just went gathering whatever we came upon for millennia before we thought of planting. It took another four thousand years before there was evidence of systematic irrigation. You would think we would have stumbled onto that idea a bit sooner. And it wasn't until five thousand years ago that we discovered that horses and oxen could pull the plow and do better hauling than poor old *homo sapiens*.[14] That's when so-called civilization got started, and cities formed after the belated discovery of other forms of power. (And I'm sure that when someone first thought of planting a seed, irrigating a field, harnessing a donkey, or making a wheel, some prehistoric administrator said, "I have never heard of such a thing!" The only answer to the administrator is, "Now that you have heard of it, can we get started?!")

For seventy-five years after the discovery that vaccination could work, no one thought of extending the idea to other diseases until Louis Pasteur in 1879. Likewise, Einstein discovered the principle of relativity based on principles that no one had taken any notice of for at least fifty years. Arthur Koestler says, "The plum was overripe, yet for half a century nobody came to pluck it." [15] Thinking ecologically, how many ripe plums are we bumping our heads against right now that no one has thought of plucking?

Even when a plum is plucked, we can refuse to take a bite. When Darwin's theory of evolution was first presented to a group of his peers, they yawned. And at the end of that year, the president of the Linnean Society, where the paper was read, wrote in his annual report that "the year which has passed . . . has not, indeed, been marked by any of those striking discoveries which at once revolutionize, so to speak, the department of science on which they bear." [16]

Some would blame earth-wrecking on high technology. An axiom of logic refutes that: *a common and constant effect points to a common and constant cause.* Before high-tech, there was us—the common and constant cause—and we were dirty low-tech mess makers also. As far back as 6000 BCE villages had to be abandoned due to soil erosion and deforestation. At about 3000 BCE Sumer became the first literate society. For a while the Sumerians thrived. Then they overwatered and salinized their fields: "The fields turned white," said a contemporary report. By 1800 BCE, Sumer's agriculture collapsed and the civilization declined into an underpopulated, impoverished backwater. The Yellow River was so called because of the amount of topsoil it carried from erosion. [17] By 312 BCE the Tiber was too polluted to drink from. And so it went. In the sixteenth century, the river Thames bristled with barbell, trout, bream, and flounder, but by the eighteenth century, all had been killed by pollution. [18]

So do we ring the death knell for the species and the

earth we have victimized? Am I writing this to unleash a wail of despair? Is there any hope?

WHAT DO CATHOLICS AND OTHER RELIGIONS HAVE TO OFFER?

At first blush, religion would seem more problem than cure. Lynn White Jr. fired a shot across the religious bow in 1967, a shot that was heard and anthologized around the world. He pinned blame on Jews and Christians because the biblical mandate to "subdue" the earth and be fruitful and multiply set the tone for environmental rape in the industrialized Christian West. While his indictment was too narrow, since there were many other culprits preaching anthropocentric hubris in the shaping of Western culture, it is true that Christians binged on species-ism. Pope John Paul II crowed, "Everything in creation is ordered to man and everything is made subject to him."[19] The pope should have paused to reflect that the fingers that held his pen were reconfigured stardust and that unto stardust they shall return. The oxygen he breathed as he wrote those proud words came from the furnaces of long-dead stars—the sources of the gases and processes that yield the bounty of oxygen. He should also have tamed his boast with a recognition that there is "no clear line between life and non-life." "The galactic story, the solar system story, the earth story, the life story, and the human story" all weave and bind into a single integral story.[20] Human royal independence from the rest of the universe is a story, but it is low-grade fiction.

Religions can contain low-grade fiction, but the high-grade stories don't lie; they reach for deeper truths about life and invite us to imagine what is possible. Flawed classics though they be, there is power in religious stories, and power is what we need. "Probably only religion has the moral force to bring about [the necessary] change," to save humanity from its self-destruction. These are the words of Jorgen Randers, commenting on the 1972 MIT report *The Limits of Growth*.[21] "Efforts to safeguard and cherish the environment need to be infused with a vision of the sacred." Those are not the words of clergy; they were written by thirty-four internationally renowned scientists led by Carl Sagan and Hans Bethe. They continued: "Problems of such magnitude, and solutions demanding so broad a perspective, must be recognized from the outset as having a religious as well as a scientific dimension."[22] Four-fifths of the world's population affiliate with one or another of the world's ten thousand religions. To ignore this force and its potential for good and for ill is the nadir of naivete.

And again, if people will die for a dogma who will not stir for a conclusion, there is going to have to be a lot of dying if the wrecking of the planet is not slowed, abated, and turned around. Even Lynn White's article indicting Jews and Christians ends with a recognition that religion must be part of the solution to the environmental crisis, and he suggests that St. Francis of Assisi, the Tuscan lover of nature, become the patron saint of ecologists.[23]

"Sacred" is the superlative of precious, and nothing, absolutely nothing, stirs the human will like the touch of the sacred.

So what have these religions to offer us in our ecological sinkhole? Can they stir us to know and feel that this earth of ours is "lovely beyond any singing of it"?[24] Could they energize us with the truth that we are, one and all, "frail, beautiful children of the universe," and in debt to it up to our necks?[25] Can they convert us from pricing to prizing? Could they help us to revel and fall in love?

Though the Bible has downers when it comes to nature, that is not the whole story. At its best, biblical joy is not a gossamer strain of otherworldly spirituality; it is rather of the earth and earthy. When the earth was made, it was pronounced "very good" (Gen. 1:31), and when it was completed, its nonworkaholic creator took a day off to rest and enjoy it (Gen. 2:2). This day off continues in the merriment of the Jewish Sabbath tradition. (Remember to thank the next Jew you meet for the weekend tradition.) Rosemary Radford Ruether hails the sabbatical legislation that mandated "periodic rest and restoration of relations between humans, animals, and land."[26] All of nature should join the dance: "Let the heavens rejoice and the earth exult, let the sea roar and all the creatures in it, let the fields exult and all that is in them; then let all the trees of the forest shout for joy" (Ps. 96:11–12). There is biblical hope even for wastelands: "Let the wilderness and the thirsty land be glad, let the desert rejoice and burst into flower" (Isa. 35:1). Water will "spring up in the wilderness, and torrents flow in dry land.

The mirage becomes a pool, the thirsty land bubbling springs" (Isa. 35:6–7).

In truth, the Bible of the Jews and Christians was not obsessed with ecology. Their main concern was with political and economic oppression and with imagining a new social order where "there shall be no poor among you" (Deut. 15:4). Still, the Hebrews were an earthy bunch, and not unmindful of the "lilies in the field" and "the birds of the air" (Matt. 6:26–28). In the Hebrew view, "all human immorality and faithlessness affect the vitality of the land itself."[27] They imagined God saying, "I am the Lord. If you follow my statutes and observe them faithfully, I will give you rain at the proper time; the land shall yield its produce and the trees of the countryside their fruit. . . . I will give peace to the land." And if they did not live morally, "I will make the sky above you like iron and the earth beneath you like bronze. . . . Your land shall not yield its produce nor the trees of the land their fruit" (Lev. 3–6;19–20). In the creation story of these people, the creator was delighted with nature and its fruitfulness, with every tree bearing fruit and the seas full of life: "God saw all that he had made and it was very good" (Gen. 1:28). When humans were told to rule over it and subdue it, it was not to be a hostile or wasteful rule. Human stewardship over the "very good" earth was to be fruitful. Otherwise, "the land shall be dried up, and all who live in it shall pine away, and with them the wild beasts and the birds of the air; even the fish shall be swept from the sea" (Hos. 4:3). Humans had it in them to wreck the earth. The Bible sounded the warning. Some evangelicals today are beginning to see this again. What a mood change it would be in America if the Christian right saw that care of the earth is a religious duty and a "family value"!

The Bible praised God for making grass for the cattle, trees for the birds, high hills for the goats, and "wine to gladden [people's] hearts" (Ps. 104:13–18).

In this, Jesus was a real Jew. No total abstainer he. He was criticized for feasting and partying while John the Baptist had fasted (Mark 2:18). "Those dinner parties were such a common feature of Jesus' life that he could be accused of being a drunkard and a glutton," writes Bible scholar and Dominican priest Albert Nolan.[28] It had to be a real challenge for old-time Methodist preachers, but the three synoptic Gospels all report that Jesus, right before his death, looked forward to having a drink in the kingdom of God! "I tell you this: never again shall I drink from the fruit of the vine until that day when I drink it new in the kingdom of God" (Matt. 26:29; Mark 14:25; Luke 22:18). Jesus attached great importance to his festive gatherings, and he wanted to be remembered in exactly that kind of context. Those who survived him were to "do this in memory" of him (1 Cor. 11:24–25).

The Bible is not abstemious in its praise of the things that bring happiness to our embodied selves. Sexual joy was applauded. The Song of Solomon is an anthology of erotic poems that picture sexual passion in luxuriant bloom without bothering with skittish details such as whether the lovers were married. Imagine! The book of Proverbs gives advice that moderns would blushingly shy from using in a wedding toast: "Have pleasure with the wife of your youth. . . . May her breasts always intoxicate you! May you ever find rapture in loving her!" (Prov. 5:18–19).

There are streams in Catholic history that harmonize with all of this. Small wonder then that Catholics such as Thomas Berry (a priest), Mary Evelyn Tucker, John Grim, and Rosemary Radford Ruether would become ecological leaders with influence well beyond Catholicism. Mary Evelyn Tucker and John Grim are the series editors at Harvard University Press for ten volumes on world religions and ecology and leaders in the United Nations Environment Programme (UNEP). Like Francis of Assisi and the Benedictine monks who championed the dignity of working with dirt, they were primed for it.[29]

Father Thomas Berry weeps at the ongoing extinctions of our kindred species of life. Nothing like it has happened since the Cenozoic era 65 million years ago. He calls for a return to the terms of the Cenozoic time, that "great lyric period in the sequence of life" when we humans first emerged into being. "Our inner world of genetic coding was shaped by these same forces that created the world about us. Our inner world is integral with this outer world. Our soul life is developed only in contact with these surrounding experiences." Our ruthless extinction of life-forms "threatens the inner life of the human along with the other biosystems of the planet."[30] As humans moved from agriculture to the "industrial non-renewing extractive economy," "the planet lost its wonder and majesty, its grace and beauty, its life-giving qualities" which are the natural source of our "spiritual identity."[31]

Rosemary Radford Ruether concurs on the spiritual anorexia that follows alienation from our matrix: "It may not be accidental that so much of the art, music, and poetry of modern urban environments is nihilistic. Without the rich beauty of the natural environment, humans may also have been losing that which has nurtured their moral aesthetic 'soul,' their sensitivity to complex and subtle realities, their capacity to imagine ecstatically and to care deeply about life."[32]

Berry departs from the *sola scriptura* theological tradition. He puts the Bible in its place. The Bible is not "our primary revelation of the Divine . . . the natural world" is. "No other revelatory experience can do for the human what the experience of the natural world does."[33] We spent too many years poring over texts and not looking out the window. Our beauty capacity is stunted. Berry says our species suffers from a self-inflicted autism, intelligent beings cut off from communion with our surroundings. Autistic children can be very intelligent, but they are detached emotionally and isolated, almost impenetrably so. We're emotionally divorced from nature. We cannot listen to the earth or "think like a mountain." Locked into ourselves, "we have broken the great conversation."[34]

Early Christianity went to bed with the Greeks and is only now recovering from that affair. The earthy wisdom that Jesus got from his Jewish forebears was invaded, as theologian Larry Rasmussen puts it, by the insidious "Platonism in which immaterial pure forms inhabit another world as true 'reality,' while the flawed one we live in is the illusory cave of shifting shadows. The earthbound is denigrated, the abstract and mathematical is elevated. Important and formative reality is put out to travel the ether on a web of its own, unencumbered by the mundane."[35] That kind of detachment melts glaciers and suffocates oceans with debris.

Father Berry does share the keen Calvinist sense of the sinful stupidity of our kind. He thinks that, like Paul, we will have to be knocked off our horse before regaining our vision. The coming end of the petroleum age (which is only a hundred years old) will shock this industrialized world, and then, it is his hope, "a new human relationship with the earth will manifest itself."[36] Berry echoes the lament of Jeremiah: "Your wrongdoing has upset nature's order, and yours sins have kept you from her kindly gifts" (Jer. 5:25).

WHAT, ME WORRY? LET GOD DO IT

Theists have a pious escape hatch when it comes to solving problems. Hamlet said it. Even when we have done our feeble best and yet, alas, "our deep plots do pall," not to worry:

> There's a divinity that shapes our ends,
> Rough-hew them how we will.
> (William Shakespeare, *Hamlet*, Act 5, Scene 2)

Muck it up we may, but our Daddy God will pick up the pieces.

This becalming confidence finds expression also in the

First Vatican Council at the end of the nineteenth century. God was seen as "protecting and governing all things" in the universe and doing so with "sweetness and with strength," *fortiter et suaviter*.[37] That doesn't quite square with the view one gets from the Hubble telescope, where the tumultuous rise and fall of stars doesn't signal that the process is under sweet management.

Interestingly, however, Catholicism in its better moments had antidotal insights on this leaving-it-to-God cop-out. Thomas Aquinas was a firm believer in God's providence. However, he insisted that humans are "participants" in this providence, not passive pawns. Being endowed with intelligence and will, it was up to us to pitch in and get the job done.[38] Catholic theology followed through on this, saying we are "co-creators" and "co-providers," not corks floating on predetermined tides. We are cooperators in the directing of those tides. On top of this, Catholic theology listed a specific sin called "tempting God," which meant shifting the burden of action onto God when we had not done all we could do. Thomas Aquinas called it a sin against religion itself. It grotesquely distorts religion to avoid our moral responsibilities.[39]

WHEN BISHOPS AWAKE

Even Catholic bishops, who are not known for innovation, are catching on to the ecological crisis—but oh so slowly. In 1975, the Catholic bishops of Appalachia published a pas-

toral letter called *The Land Is Home to Me*. This letter celebrated "the precious mountain spirit" of the mountain people and "their oneness with the rest of nature." Catholics
don't always devour letters from bishops, but this one sold a
quarter of a million copies. They followed up in 1995 with *At
Home in the Web of Life*. The very sensible theme of this letter is: "Human dignity and community are linked with the
wider dignity and community of nature in the single web of
life." [40]

Distracted as our bishops have been with pelvic issues
and churchy problems, this initiative has not burgeoned into
a movement. That's a shame, because bishops have great
leadership potential. Think of it. Bishops are theater. They
are opera, and people like a bit of pomp and circumstance.
(President Carter dropped, but then had to restore, "Hail to
the Chief"; the people required it.) When a Catholic bishop
arrives at his new diocese, it is high drama. He arrives at the
cathedral bedecked in medieval grandeur, with a towering
miter on his head and a gilded crozier staff in his hand. When
he reaches the cathedral door, the door is ceremonially
closed to him. He has to knock with his crozier, and only
when he is received by the waiting throng does that door
open to the sound of trumpets and song.

Compare that to the arrival of the new Protestant church
leader. His reception is likely to be orderly and therefore
dull. No pizzazz. The pope and the Dalai Lama have pizzazz.
They can go anywhere in the world and get a hearing. Bishops united on ecology as a family value could bring earth into
the equation when politicians speak of "moral values." Again,

when Cardinal Mahoney spoke out against pending legislation against illegal immigrants, he said that if the legislation
passed as such, he would tell his priests to disobey the law in
their service of the poor immigrants. That intervention
changed the discourse in Washington. If bishops spoke with
passion and acuity on real issues, they would get a hearing.
People hunger for inspired leadership and there is none, and
where there is none, lies are king.

BUT WHAT ABOUT POPULATION PRESSURE, BIRTH CONTROL, AND ABORTION?

Before moving to the remedial power of Catholic earthiness,
let's go to that bone that still sticks in the Catholic throat—or,
more accurately, in some Catholic throats and most bishops'
throats. The question has to be asked: can you put Catholic
and ecological good sense in the same sentence? Catholics
are said to oppose all birth control and abortion when
needed as a backup.

That's a great big lie.

The Roman Catholic position on abortion is pluralistic
and always has been. It has a strong prochoice tradition
alongside a no-choice position, and neither position is more
official or more Catholic than the other. Just as there is a
just-war theory espoused by some Catholics, there is a "just-
abortion theory" espoused by many Catholic experts and lay
people. The Catholic prochoice position, defended for centuries by saints and scholars, was hidden in the attic lest the
kids find it. But scholarship has outed it. (If bishops don't

know that, there is a cure for their ignorance: they can be sent back to school.)

As a sampler of the long Catholic prochoice tradition, let's take one saint and one Jesuit theologian from the heretofore hidden Catholic historical treasury.

Saint Antoninus! Not much heard of anymore: you don't meet many Antoninus O'Briens, and more's the pity. He is not prayed to before Notre Dame football games, even though, who knows, he might even help them win a bowl game. But saint he is—canonized in 1523—and solidly prochoice for early abortions when necessary to save the life of the woman, which was not at all a rarity given the medical conditions of his time. Antoninus was a Dominican monk who became the archbishop of Florence, where his body lies today in repose. Antoninus's prochoice view was commonplace, stirred no controversy, and was not seen as an obstacle to his formal canonization.

Before pontificating on the "immorality" of all abortions, Catholic bishops should pause and say a little prayer to this saintly prochoice predecessor. Indeed, if I could get a grant, I would commission statues of this holy man and send them to all the Catholic bishops in the world, with an extra large one (out of respect) going to the pope. It would be a lovely reminder of the variety and richness of the Catholic tradition of respect for women.

For a theologian, I can choose out of many, for example, Jesuit Tomas Sanchez (1550–1610). One of the traditional Catholic sources of truth was the *auctores probati*, the tested

authors, the theologians whose work was so thoroughly en-
dorsed by peers and lay people that it became a reliable authority. One of the most tested and most esteemed in the
tradition was Tomas Sanchez and his classic text *De Sancto
Matrimonii Sacramento*. Sanchez approved of early abortions when necessary (a) to save the life of the mother,
(b) when a woman was pregnant from one man but about to
be married to another, or (c) when relatives might kill the
woman if they found out she was pregnant. Also, bad medical
science in his day said intercourse in early pregnancy could
cause abortions. Even so, Sanchez said it was moral to have
intercourse during pregnancy since the moral status of the
early fetus was not "such a great loss." It did not have personal status; it was human tissue, but it was not a person.

Saints Augustine and Thomas Aquinas held that the
early fetus had the moral status of a plant or vegetable. As it
matured it had the equivalent of the soul of an animal. Only
when it was formed could it receive a human soul and be a
person. Augustine believed in the resurrection of all the dead
of history at the end of time. When asked if aborted fetuses
would rise at that time, he said no. They had not reached personal status. He added that all the sperm of history would not
rise either, and for that we can be grateful. One would hate to
see the saints on such a glorious occasion slipping and sliding
around on all that resurrected sperm.[41]

On contraception, many bishops have left Vatican theology for the broader and richer Catholic theology. When Pope
Paul VI condemned all artificial contraception in 1968, the

national conferences of Catholic bishops "in fourteen different nations issued pastoral letters assuring their laity that
those who could not in good faith accept this teaching were
not sinners."[42] As we noted in chapter 1, in Maputo, Mozambique, in 2003, the Catholic bishop was asked in his HIV-
ravaged diocese about the use of condoms. He said: "You see,
if you are HIV positive and you have unprotected sex and you
infect someone, you have, in the eyes of God, committed
murder. Or if you are HIV negative and you have unprotected sex with someone who is infected, and they infect you,
you have, in the eyes of God, committed suicide. So my children, wearing a condom is not a sin—not wearing one is!"
Reality in; Vatican theology out. Catholics growing up.

CATHOLICS FALLING IN LOVE

The late Harvard biologist Stephen Jay Gould said that we
need "an emotional/spiritual bond between ourselves and
nature" since "we will not fight to save what we do not love."[43]
The renewable moral energies of the Catholic traditions are
turning toward a celebration of this earth and the gift it is.

There is something in Catholicism that makes it a natural
for adaptation to earth consciousness, and that adaptation is
starting. Catholics have always believed the icon to be mightier than the word. Catholics, warmed for centuries by
Mediterranean breezes, combined sensuousness with spirituality. Witness the repertoire of earthy elements in Catholic
worship: water, oil, wine, bread, salt, wax, fire, ashes, incense,

vestments, touching, music. Catholics sought the invisible sacred through the visible world, *invisibilia per visibilia*, as they sang it in their liturgy. At a time when the body—especially the female body—was despised in the fog of a *fuga mundi* ("flight from the world") spirituality, these people took a body, a woman's body, and imagined it elevated into the holy of holies: the poetic portrayal of the Assumption of Mary's body into heaven.

There were strong strains in the Catholic tradition that can be absolved from Wendell Berry's critique of those Christians with world-eschewing spiritualities who are bent on "incanting anemic souls into Heaven."[44] Hilaire Belloc swam in this Catholic stream when he wrote:

Wherever a Catholic sun doth shine
There's lots of laughter and good red wine!
At least I've always found it so.
Benedicamus Domino!

Let's face it. Calvinists never produced a liqueur like the Benedictine monks did, much less a Christian Brothers brandy. Nor do their rituals contain a *benedictio cervesiae*, a holy blessing of beer.

Maybe a "b" word is at the heart of the renewable strengths of the Catholic traditions. The word is *beauty*. A passion for it is at the root of Catholic cathedral-building compulsion and liturgical pomp as well as its earthiness and sensuousness, all the way from the heights of ritual down to the blessing of beer. Our spirits need sensual richness and beauty like our lungs need oxygen. Catholic earthy hungers need stoking. It is these exuberant, imagination-driving hungers—not contorted dogmas and authoritarian potentates——that would be the best Catholic gift to a world that has lost its capacity to look around and say "Wow!"

Acknowledgments

Catholic liturgical services tend to begin with a confession of faults and sin. Not a bad idea, since we don't like facing up to our downside. But better yet is the Native American practice of beginning liturgies with gratitude. Let me end this book that way, gratefully, heartily so.

My thanks go to parents who raised me in a peaceful home where laughter always had the right of way. They and my dynamic siblings lived through my many changes—some painful to them—and they did so generously.

I'm grateful to students whose questions often opened new horizons and stunned me with what I had been missing.

I'm grateful to teachers, especially those at Rome's venerable Gregorian University. They introduced me to Greek, Roman, Hebrew, and Christian classics. They might not all be happy today with where I've gone with those treasures, but they were scholars who gave me a passion for the patient and disciplined pursuit of truth.

I'm thankful to Thomas Aquinas, who got me out of a lot of trouble over the years. Some Irish priests who were my students at the Catholic University of America were once spoofing the faculty at a party. Their bit on me:

Apparently Aquinas is not so bad at all
'Cause Dan always quotes him when his back's against
    the wall.

Thomas Aquinas, for all his blind spots, was a rebel in his day. Small wonder he became his time's most heavily censured intellectual, reading forbidden pagans like Aristotle and others and bringing them into medieval discourse.

I thank my son Tom, named for Thomas Aquinas and possessed of a similar mind, sharp and independent; grateful memories go to my son Danny, a life too soon ended, who still fills my thoughts and pages.

I give thanks to the people of Planned Parenthood, who taught me how hard it is to receive honors from people who deserve more honor than you do. They have given me awards and invited me to present keynote addresses at the annual events of at least a third of their 130 affiliates. And at those sessions I got as much as I gave. They do not work in the placid groves of academe. There was always police protection at their events. When I spoke at the convention of abortion providers, the National Abortion Federation, bomb-sniffing dogs had to test each room and each speaker's rostrum before we could enter. Because these professionals serve women and are often the only source of medical care for poor women, they face threats and insults on a daily basis. They have the rare virtue of courage in a land where the

ACKNOWLEDGMENTS 161

toady is king. Being with them has always infused the blood of hope into my veins.

I am grateful to Marquette University. Its president, John Raynor, SJ, was confronted by a prospective big donor right after I was hired there. My hiring had been written up in *Time* magazine and the donor asked, "Why should I give you money when you have just hired this liberal professor?" Father Raynor's reply: "Maguire's head is not for sale. He has the credentials we want." (He got the money anyhow, I am relieved to say.) But his words underline the support for my academic freedom that Marquette has given almost perfectly for thirty-five years.

I am grateful to the eleventh- and twelfth-century Christians who pioneered the idea of the university as a place, in Cardinal Newman's phrase, "where many minds compete freely together." Each word of that phrase is a pearl of great price.

I am in debt, as are all American scholars, to the American Association of University Professors for their untiring defense of tenure and academic freedom. Without them, petty controllers would quickly undermine the integrity of our searching.

I thank Rita Nakashima Brock, who told me I was dead wrong when I said I was too busy to do this book. She is gifted with communicable enthusiasm for the good, the true, and the beautiful, and I am happily in her debt.

And I thank The New Press for taking religion seriously, seeing it as a ubiquitous power for good or for ill, a power that is never quiescent or lacking in influence. They saw the need to energize the religious left, who have been out-shouted and eclipsed by the fear-driven right, so much so that many people don't even know we are here!

Anger is a wonderful virtue when justice and the love of truth are its goads, but gratitude is its gentle civilizer, as is humor, and I thank all who have nourished both along the trail of my life.

Notes

INTRODUCTION

1. Sam Harris, *The End of Faith: Religion, Terror, and the Future of Reason* (New York: W.W. Norton & Co., 2004), 12.

2. See Harold Coward and Daniel C. Maguire, *Visions of a New Earth: Religious Perspectives on Population, Consumption, and Ecology* (Albany: State University of New York Press, 2000), 1–13.

3. Huston Smith, *The Religions of Man* (New York: Harper & Row Perennial Library, 1965), 11.

4. Garry Wills, "Faith and the Race for God and Country," *Sojourners* 15 (March 14, 1988), 4–5.

5. Edward Luttwak, "The Missing Dimension," in *Religion: The Missing Dimension of Statecraft*, ed. Douglas Johnston and Cynthia Sampson. (New York: Oxford University Press, 1994), 8–9.

6. H. Hendricks, *The Infancy Narratives* (London: Chapman, 1984), 84. See Luke 1:46–55. See Daniel C. Maguire, "Justice Bible-Style," in *A Moral Creed for All Christians* (Minneapolis: Fortress Press, 2005), 41–80.

7. Emil Brunner, *Justice and the Social Order* (London: Lutterworth, 1945), 7.

CHAPTER 1: GOOD SEX

1. See Marie M. Fortune, *Love Does No Harm: Sexual Ethics for the Rest of Us* (New York: Continuum, 1995), 116–18. Fortune

writes: "Interestingly, throughout the Song of Solomon there is no mention of procreative purpose nor are the woman and the man described as being married. There is no suggestion of a dominant/submissive relationship, but rather a peer relationship: 'This is my beloved and this is my friend. . . .' (5:16). The entire poem describes recreative sex with the singular purpose of sharing the passion and pleasure of a relationship between equals. It is tragic that this pleasure-affirming aspect of the Hebrew tradition has been lost or withheld from Christianity for so long" (p. 118).

2. See Garry Wills, *Saint Augustine,* Penguin Lives series (New York: Lipper/Viking, 1999).

3. Augustine, *City of God,* 14.24.

4. In what amounts to a textbook of Christian sexual pathology, Uta Ranke Heinnemann chronicles the attitudes that suffused Christian history in her *Eunuchs for the Kingdom of Heaven: Women, Sexuality, and the Catholic Church* (New York: Doubleday, 1990).

5. E. H. Harte, "Masturbatory Insanity: The History of an Idea," *Journal of Mental Science* 108 (January 1962) 1–25.

6. Ibid.

7. Edward O. Laumann et al., *The Social Organization of Sexuality: Sexual Practices in the United States* (Chicago: University of Chicago Press, 1994), 115.

8. Patricia Koch and David Weise, eds., *Sexuality in America* (New York: Continuum, 1999), 228, 114. See also Debra W. Haffner, *Beyond the Big Talk: Every Parent's Gudie to Raising Sexually Healthy Teens* (New York: Newmarket Press, 2001).

9. See Jasmine Karalakulasingam, "Study Challenges Abstinence: Teen Pregnancy Drop Due to Safer Sex, Not No Sex," *Independent* (UK) (December 5, 2006), www.religiousconsultation.org. On the United States and other industrialized countries see

Teenage Pregancy in Industrialized Countries (New Haven, CT: Yale University Press, 1986).

10. "Believe It or Not": Spirituality Is the New Religion," *Mother Jones* (November/December 1997).

11. Joyce Lain Kennedy, "Spirituality, Change of Focus Can Revitalize Your Attitude About Work," *Milwaukee Journal Sentinel* (June 6, 1999).

12. Kiddushin 66d, quoted by William E. Phipps, *Was Jesus Married?: The Distortion of Sexuality in the Christian Tradition* (New York: Harper & Row, 1970), 16.

13. Daniel A. Dombrowski and Robert Deltete, *A Brief, Liberal, Catholic Defense of Abortion* (Urbana and Chicago: University of Illinois Press, 2000), 86.

14. David Patient, http://archives.healthdev.net/af-aids. See also www.religiousconsultation.org.

15. Laurie Goering, "South African Bishop Bucks Vatican on Condom Use," *Chicago Tribune* (November 4, 2005).

16. For all these references and for others in a similar vein, see Patricia Beattie Jung, Mary E. Hunt, and Radhika Balakrishnan, eds., *Good Sex: Feminist Perspectives from the World's Religions* (New Brunswick, NJ: Rutgers University Press, 2000).

CHAPTER 2: MALE AND FEMALE WERE WE MADE

1. A.Y. Lewin and L. Duchan et al., "Letters," *Science* 176 (1972), 457–59.

2. John T. Pawlikowski, "Human Rights in the Roman Catholic Tradition," in *American Society of Christian Ethics, Selected Papers, 1979*, ed. Max L. Stackhouse (Waterloo, ON: Council on the Study of Religion, 1979), 153.

3. Ibid.

4. Kenneth Grayston, "Marriage," in *A Theological Word Book*

of the Bible, ed. Alan Richardson (New York: Macmillan, 1963), 139. Grayston refers to Genesis 16:1ff and 30:1ff.

5. Augustine, *On Genesis According to the Letter*, 9–7 (Vienna: Corpus Scriptorum Ecclesiasticorum, 1866), 28:275.

6. See Elisabeth Schussler Fiorenza, *In Memory of Her: A Feminist Theological Reconstruction of Christian Origins* (New York: Crossroad, 1983).

7. Sam Harris, *The End of Faith: Religion, Terror, and the Future of Reason* (New York: W.W. Norton & Co., 2004).

8. Ibid., 129.

9. C.H. Dodd, *The Founder of Christianity* (New York: Macmillan, 1970), 64.

10. Abraham Heschel, *The Prophets* (New York: Harper & Row, 1962), 198.

11. Robert Jewett and John Shelton Lawrence, *Captain America and the Crusade Against Evil: The Dilemma of Zealous Nationalism* (Grand Rapids, MI: W.B. Eerdmans, 2003).

12. John W. Dixon Jr., "The Erotics of Knowing," *Anglican Theological Review* 56 (January 1974), 8.

13. Carol Gilligan, "Moral Development," *Harvard Educational Review* 47 (November 1977), 482.

14. Ibid.

15. Bernadette J.W.T. Brooten, *Love Between Women: Early Christian Responses to Female Homoeroticism* (Chicago: University of Chicago Press, 1996), 189–90.

16. Ibid.

17. Bruce Bagemihl, *Biological Exuberance: Animal Homosexuality and Natural Diversity* (New York: St. Martin's Press, 1999), 37.

18. John Boswell, *Same-Sex Unions in Premodern Europe* (New York: Vintage Books, 1995), 193.

19. See Walter M. Abbott, ed., "Dogmatic Constitution on the

Church," in *The Documents of Vatican II* (New York: Herder and Herder, 1966), 71.

20. William Sloane Coffin, "Diversity and Inclusion," *Mount Holyoke Alumnae Quarterly* (Winter 1999), 23.

CHAPTER 3: THE PERENNIAL ORPHANS
OF AMERICAN CONSCIENCE

1. James Baldwin, "An Open Letter to My Sister, Angela Davis," quoted in Derrick A. Bell Jr., "Racism in American Courts: Cause for Black Disruption or Despair?" *California Law Review* 61 (January 1973), 203.

2. Derrick Bell, "The Real Cost of Racial Equality," *Civil Liberties Review Survey* (Summer 1974), 97.

3. Quoted in David McCullough, *John Adams* (New York: Simon & Schuster, 2001), 331.

4. Quoted in Howard Zinn, *A People's History of the United States, 1492–Present,* revised and updated edition (New York: Harper Perennial, 1995), 183–84.

5. Gerald David Jaynes and Robin M. Williams Jr., eds., *A Common Destiny: Blacks and American Society* (Washington, DC: National Academy Press, 1989), 398–403.

6. Kevin Phillips, *American Theocracy* (New York: Viking, 2006), 123. Amazingly, there are hundreds of thousands of African American Catholics who were attracted to Catholicism and were able to overlook the racist record of the American Catholic Church.

7. U.S. Conference of Catholic Bishops, http://www.nccfuscc.org/saac/bishopspastoral.shtml.

8. See Daniel C. Maguire, *A New American Justice: Ending the White Male Monopolies* (Garden City, NY: Doubleday & Co., 1980); Daniel C. Maguire, *A Case for Affirmative Action* (Dubuque, IA: Shepherd, 1982).

9. Alice Rivlin, testimony before the Joint Economics Committee, *Thirtieth Anniversary of the Employment Act of 1946—A National Conference on Full Employment* (Washington, DC: Government Printing Office, 1976), 276. See also Gar Alperovitz, "Planning for Sustained Community," in *Catholic Social Teaching and the United States Economy*, ed. John W. Houck and Oliver F. Williams (Washington, DC: University Press of America, 1984), 331–58.

10. Clearly, the "neoliberal" and "neoconservative" philosophies that have been guiding American capitalism do not move toward full employment. As Juliet Schor says, "The U.S. economy is increasingly unable to provide work for its population"—at least work that will lift people out of poverty. See Juliet Schor, *The Overworked American: The Unexpectd Decline of Leisure* (New York: Basic Books, 1991), 39. Outsourcing, foreign and internal "sweatshops," and the forced employment of children worldwide are all tools of neoslavery, to stick to the "neo" jargon du jour. See Mary Elizabeth Hobgood, *Dismantling Privilege: An Ethics of Accountability* (Cleveland: Pilgrim Press, 2000).

11. Bell, "The Real Cost of Racial Equality," 94.

12. Arthur Ashe and Arnold Rampersad, "The Burden of Race," *Long-Term View* 2, no. 4 (Fall 1994), 23.

13. Ibid., 24.

14. Gloria H. Albrecht, *Hitting Home: Feminist Ethics, Women's Work, and the Betrayal of "Family Values"* (New York: Continuum, 2002), 58.

15. "Whiteness Studies," http://www.startribune.com/462/story/667886.html, September 11, 2006. This is a report on a working paper by Paul R. Croll, Douglas Hartman, and Joseph Gerteis, "Putting Whiteness Theory to the Test: An Empirical Assessment of Core Theoretical Propositions." Contact: crol0004@umn.edu.

16. Vivian Verdell Gordon and Lois Smith Owens, "The Dilemma Continues," *Long-Term View* 2, no. 4 (Fall 1994), 34.

17. Albrecht, *Hitting Home*, 46–47.

18. Hobgood, *Dismantling Privilege*, 104. See Carolyn Howe, *Political Ideology and Class Formation: A Study of the Middle Class* (Westport, CT: Praeger, 1992).

CHAPTER 4: WAR IS FOR DUMMIES

1. Michael Walzer, *Just and Unjust Wars* (New York: Basic Books, 1977), 36.

2. J. Glenn Gray, *The Warriors: Reflections on Men in Battle* (New York: Basic Books, 1977), 36.

3. Barbara Ehrenreich, *Blood Rites: Origins and History of the Passions of War* (New York: Henry Holt & Co., 1998), 175–78.

4. Jerome D. Frank, *Sanity and Survival: Psychological Aspects of War and Peace* (New York: Vintage Books, 1968), 134–35.

5. "The World at War, January 2002," *Defense Monitor* 31, no. 1 (January 2002).

6. Jonathan Schell, *The Unconquerable World* (New York: Henry Holt & Co., 2003), 3.

7. Ehrenreich, *Blood Rites*, 7.

8. Ibid.

9. Erich Fromm, *The Anatomy of Human Destructiveness* (New York: Holt, Rinehart & Winston, 1973), 105.

10. Kevin Phillips, *American Theocracy* (New York: Viking, 2006), 100.

11. Reinhold Niebuhr spoke of "the feeble mind of a nation" in his *Moral Man and Immoral Society* (New York: Charles Scribner's Sons, 1960 edition), 88—not just this American nation but all collectivities. The term is apt. As we collectivize into nations we get discoordinated and dumber and do things that would get an individual committed to an institution that treats mental illness.

12. Tertullian, *Idolatry*, XIX.

13. Lactantius, *The Divine Institutes*, VI, xx. 15–16.

14. Augustine, *Epistles*, 138, ii.14.

15. *Dictionaire de Theologie Catholique*, vol. 6, col. 1920.

16. See Daniel C. Maguire, *The New Subversives: Anti-Americanism of the Religious Right* (New York: Continuum, 1982), chapter 4, "The Amnesia of the New Right."

17. Stanley Windass, *Christianity vs. Violence* (London: Sheed & Ward, 1964), 43.

18. *Calvini Opera, Corpus Reformatorum* VIII, 476; XXIV, 360; XLIV 346.

19. Walter Wink, *Jesus and Nonviolence: A Third Way* (Minneapolis: Fortress, 2003), 1–2.

20. See Karen Armstrong, *The Battle for God* (New York: Random House, 2001), vii.

21. Richard Falk, "Why International Law Matters," *Nation* 276 (March 10, 2003), 20.

22. Anne Frank, *The Diary of a Young Girl*, trans. B. M. Mooyaart (Garden City, NY: Doubleday, 1953), 201.

23. Bruce Russett, in *Just Peacemaking: Ten Practices for Abolishing War*, ed. Glenn Stassen (Cleveland: Pilgrim Press, 1998). See also Daniel C. Maguire, "The Abnormality of War: Dissecting the 'Just War' Euphemisms and Building an Ethics of Peace," *Horizons* 33 (Spring 2006), 111–26.

24. Howard Zinn, *A People's History of the United States: 1492 to the Present* (New York: Harper Perennial, 1995), 75–76.

25. Desmond Tutu, "Stop Killing the Children," *Washington Post* (November 24, 1996).

26. Another Catholic staple, "the principle of double effect," is used and abused to beat the rap on the slaughter of civilians. The core insight is simple enough: we often do good things that have bad effects. So, we remove a cancerous uterus, with two effects, one good (the cancer is gone) and one bad (the woman is infertile). The principle of double effect sought to answer the question of moral responsibility for that bad effect. The answer was, you are

not responsible as long as you did not really want that bad effect and as long as there was proportionality between the effects. When the principle goes to war, all limits melt. It has been used to say that we can bomb hospital ships with wounded on board lest the enemy use the ship later for military purposes. And it was used to justify obliteration bombing in World War II, saying we did not intend the death of the population, we just wanted to knock out a factory or two. All the refinements of this ethical principle are crushed by "military necessity" and the fraud that war spawns.

27. S. V. Viswanatha, *International Law in Ancient India* (Bombay, 1925), 156, quoted in Walzer, *Just and Unjust Wars*, 43.

28. Joseph Fahey, *War and Christian Conscience* (Maryknoll, NY: Orbis Books, 2005), 110.

29. Andrew J.W.T. Bacevich, *The New American Militarism: How Americans Are Seduced by War* (New York and London: Oxford University Press, 2005). See also Drew Christiansen, "Catholic Peacemaking, 1991–2005: The Legacy of Pope John Paul II," *Review of Faith and International Affairs* 4, no. 3 (Fall 2006), 21–28.

CHAPTER 5: UPWARDLY MOBILE POVERTY

1. Howard Zinn, *A People's History of the United States: 1492 to the Present* (New York: Harper Perennial, 1995), 83.

2. Ibid., 84.

3. Quoted by Barbara Ehrenreich and Tamara Draut, "Downsized But Not Out," *Nation* (November 6, 2006), 5.

4. Quoted in Barbara Hilkert Andolsen, *The New Job Contract: Economic Justice in an Age of Insecurity* (Cleveland: Pilgrim Press, 1998), 95.

5. William Greider, "Riding into the Sunset," *Nation* (June 27, 2005), 17.

6. See Walter L. Owensby, *Economics for Prophets: A Primer on Concepts, Realities, and Values in Our Economic System* (Grand Rapids, MI: W.B. Eerdmans, 1988), and Herbert Gans, *The War Against the Poor* (New York: Basic Books, 1945).

7. See Gans, *War Against the Poor*; David K. Shipler, *The Working Poor: Invisible in America* (New York: Alfred A. Knopf, 2004); Loretta Schwartz-Nobel, *Growing Up Empty* (New York: HarperCollins, 2002); Daniel C. Maguire, "Poverty, Population, and Sustainable Development," in *Interfaith Reflections on Women, Poverty, and Population*" (Washington, DC: Centre for Development and Population Activities, 1996), 44–52.

8. Gloria Albrecht, *Hitting Home* (New York: Continuum, 2002), 79.

9. Alexander Keyssar, "Reminders of Poverty, Soon Forgotten," *Chronicle of Higher Education* (November 4, 2005), B8.

10. Mimi Abramovitz, *Under Attack, Fighting Back: Women and Welfare in the United States* (New York: Monthly Review Press, 2000), 37–39.

11. Michael Harrington, "Jobs, Not Welfare," *New York Times* (February 5, 1987), Op-Ed.

12. Kim Philips-Fein, "The Education of Jessica Rivera," *Nation* (November 25, 2002), 20.

13. Ibid., 21.

14. Ehrenreich and Draut, "Downsized," 4–5. The authors have organized a group called United Professionals, a broad-based organization for the white-collar unemployed, underemployed, and anxiously employed. They point out that many members of the "knowledge economy" hover just inches above the working poor. They sink further as gaps in their employment record turn off prospective employers.

15. Leonard Goodwin, *Do the Poor Want to Work? A Social-Psychological Study of Work Orientations* (Washington, DC: Brookings Institution, 1972), 112.

16. Susan George, "A Short History of Neoliberalism," in *The Other Davos Summit: The Globalization of Resistance to the World Economic System*, ed. François Houtart and François Polet (London and New York: Zed Books, 2001), 7–16.

17. Nancy Folbre, *The Invisible Heart: Economics and Family Values* (New York: The New Press, 2001), 131–35.

18. Albrecht, *Hitting Home*, 82.

19. Elizabeth Olson, "U.N. Surveys Paid Leave for Mothers," *New York Times* (February 16, 1998), A5.

20. Edmund L. Andrews, "Germany Weighs Overhaul of 'Consensus' Capitalism," *New York Times* (February 14, 2001), W1, W7; Edmund L. Andrews, "Europe Toughens Up on Job Cuts," *New York Times* (December 1, 2001), C1, C3.

21. Albrecht, *Hitting Home*, 130, n. 18.

22. Steven Greenhouse, "Report Shows Americans Have More 'Labor Days,' " *New York Times* (September 5, 1999), 1WK, 4WK.

23. Quoted in Owensby, *Economics for Prophets*, 77.

24. Katrina Vanden Heuvel, "$13,700 an Hour," *Nation* (May 1, 2006), 5–6.

25. Quoted in Zinn, *A People's History*, 83.

26. Mary Elizabeth Hobgood, *Dismantling Privilege: An Ethics of Accountability* (Cleveland: Pilgrim Press, 2000), 82.

27. For more on the left-wing views that are central to the Bible, see Daniel C. Maguire, *A Moral Creed for All Christians* (Minneapolis: Fortress Press, 2005), chapters 4 and 5.

28. Glenn Feldman, "Unholy Alliance: Suppressing Catholic Teachings in Subservience to Republican Ascendance in America," *Political Theology* (online).

29. Andolsen, *New Job Contract*, 106.

30. Pope Leo XIII, *Rerum Novarum* (1891), paragraph 2.

31. Ibid., paragraph 29.

32. Ibid., paragraph 34. Leo remained a social conservative in

that he accepted patriarchal and class hierarchy assumptions. Still, he was sensitive to the exploited poor.

33. Ibid., paragraph 17.

34. Pope John Paul II, *Laborem Exercens* (1981), paragraph 8.

35. Pope John Paul II, "Opening Address at the Puebla Conference," in *Puebla and Beyond: Documentation and Commentary,* ed. John Eagleson and Philip Scharper (Maryknoll, NY: Orbis Books, 1980), 67.

36. "Is Liberal Capitalism the Only Path?" *Origens* 20 (May 24, 1990), 20.

37. Pope Paul VI, *Octogesimo Adveniens* (1971), paragraph 23.

38. *Economic Justice for All: Pastoral Letter on Catholic Social Teaching and the U.S. Economy* (Washington, DC: United States Catholic Conference, Inc., 1986), paragraph 60.

39. Clive Ponting, *A Green History of the World: The Environment and the Collapse of Great Civilizations* (New York: Penguin Books, 1991), 254.

40. Clyde Prestowitz, *Rogue Nation: American Unilateralism and the Failure of Good Intentions* (New York: Basic Books, 2003), 26.

41. "Military Spending: CDI Analysts Take a Close Look at Defense Budgets," *Defense Monitor* 31, no. 2 (March–April 2006). My figures are not exaggerated. The 2007 proposed federal budget asked for $513 billion for the military, but only $1.3 billion for energy and $86 billion for education.

CHAPTER 6: EARTH THREATS, EARTH HOPES

1. See http://en.wikipedia.org/wiki/Larry_Walters. Books and articles proliferated about Larry, and he made the rounds of the big talk shows. He even did a stint as a motivational speaker. He shot himself to death in the Angeles National Forest in Southern Cali-

fornia on October 6, 1993, thus tragically becoming perhaps even more of a symbol of our age.

2. Clive Ponting, *A Green History of the World: The Environment and the Collapse of Great Civilizations* (New York: Penguin Books, 1991), 374.

3. David W. Orr, *Earth in Mind: On Education, Environment, and the Human Prospect* (Washington, DC, and Covelo, CA: Island Press, 1994).

4. Duane Elgin, *Promise Ahead: A Vision of Hope and Action for Humanity's Future* (New York: William Morrow, 2000), 26–28.

5. John Tuxill and Chris Bright, "Losing Strands in the Web of Life," in *State of the World, 1998* (New York: W.W. Norton, 1998), 42.

6. Edward O. Wilson, *The Future of Life* (New York: Alfred A. Knopf, 2002), 121.

7. Henry Parks Wright, ed., *Juvenal* (Boston: Ginn & Company, 1901), 77–89. *"Duas tantum res anxius optat, panem et circenses."* (Two things only do the anxious people want, bread and circuses.)

8. Ponting, *A Green History*, 1–7.

9. Clyde Prestowitz, *Rogue Nation: American Unilateralism and the Failure of Good Intentions* (New York: Basic Books, 2003), 111.

10. Quoted in Goran Moller, *Ethics and the Life of Faith: A Christian Moral Perspective* (Leuven, Belgium: Peeters, 1998), 35.

11. See Daniel C. Maguire, *A Moral Creed for All Christians* (Minneapolis: Fortress Press, 2005), 3–4.

12. Quoted in Elizabeth Kolbert, "Annals of Science: The Climate of Man—III," *New Yorker* (May 9, 2005), 57.

13. Ponting, *A Green History*, 254.

14. Arnold J. Toynbee, *Change and Habit: The Challenge of Our Time* (New York: Oxford University Press, 1966), 77, 21. After

900,000 years of fooling around, Toynbee notes that "at the dawn of civilization, Man reinforced his own muscle-power with animal muscle-power by domesticating the donkey, and he discovered how to travel on water, as well as overland, by inventing boats and learning to harness wind-power to propel them with sails."

15. Arthur Koestler, *The Act of Creation* (New York: Dell Publishing Co., Laurel edition, 1967), 111.

16. Quoted ibid., 142.

17. Ponting, *A Green History*, 69–74.

18. Ibid., 348, 361.

19. Pope John Paul II, *The Gospel of Life* (New York: Random House, 1995), 60–61, 149.

20. Larry L. Rasmussen, *Earth Community, Earth Ethics* (Maryknoll, NY: Orbis Books, 1996), 325.

21. Jorgen Randers, "Ethical Limitations and Human Responsibilities," in *To Create a Different Future: Religious Hope and Technological Plannning*, ed. Kenneth Vaux (New York: Friendship Press, 1972), 32; Donella H. Meadows et al., *The Limits to Growth: A Report on the Club of Rome's Project on the Predicament of Mankind* (New York: Universe Books, 1972).

22. "An Open Letter to the Religious Community," 3. The letter is available from the National Religious Partnership for the Environment, 1047 Amsterdam Ave., New York, NY 10025.

23. Lynn White, "The Historical Roots of Our Ecological Crisis," in *This Sacred Earth: Religion, Nature, Environment*, ed. Roger S. Gottlieb (New York: Routledge, 1996), 184–93.

24. Alan Paton, *Cry the Beloved Country* (New York: Scribner's, 1948), 3.

25. Rasmussen, *Earth Community*, 353.

26. Rosemary Radford Ruether, "Conclusion," in *Christianity and Ecology: Seeking the Well-Being of Earth and Humans*, ed. Dieter T. Hessel and Rosemary Radford Ruether (Cambridge, MA: Harvard University Press, 2000), 607.

27. Rasmussen, *Earth Community*, 250.

28. Albert Nolan, *Jesus Before Christianity* (Minneapolis: Fortress Press, 1978), 38.

29. Rosemary Radford Ruether writes: "Monastic communities in western Europe not only were centers for the preservation of literary culture, but they also created a new union of subsistence agriculture with egalitarian spiritual community. St. Benedict united intellect and labor by decreeing that monks do their own domestic and agricultural work." She also notes that wealth later corrupted the monasteries, when the monks brought in serf labor to increase affluence. *Corruptio optimi pessima*: the corruption of that which is best is the worst. See Rosemary Radford Ruether, *Gaia & God: An Ecofeminist Theology of Earth Healing* (San Francisco: HarperCollins, 1992), 188.

30. Thomas Berry, "Christianity's Role in the Earth Project," in *Christianity and Ecology*, Hessel and Ruether, eds., 127–28.

31. Ibid., 128–30.

32. Ruether, *Gaia & God*, 102.

33. Berry, "Christianity's Role in the Earth Project," 133, 131.

34. Thomas Berry with Thomas Clarke S.J., *Befriending the Earth* (Mystic, CT: Twenty-Third Press, 1991), 97.

35. Rasmussen, *Earth Community*, 71.

36. Berry, 134.

37. *Constitutio Dogmatica de Fide Catholica*, chapter 1.

38. Thomas Aquinas, *Summa Theologiae*, I II, q. 91, a. 2. The human person is *providentiae particeps, sibi ipsi et aliis providens*: a participant in providence who must provide for self and for others.

39. Ibid., II, q. 97, a.3.

40. Copies can be obtained at the Catholic Committee of Appalachia, P.O. Box 662, Webster Springs, WV 26288; phone and fax, 304-847-7215.

41. See Daniel C. Maguire, *Sacred Choices: The Right to Con-*

traception and Abortion in Ten World Religions (Minneapolis: Fortress Press, 2001); Daniel C. Maguire, ed., *Sacred Rights: The Case for Contraception and Abortion in World Religions* (New York: Oxford University Press, 2003). Catholic scholars from the Jesuit Seattle University show the strength of the Catholic pro-choice tradition in their *A Brief, Liberal, Catholic Defense of Abortion* (Urbana and Chicago: University of Illinois Press, 2000).

42. Christine Gudorf, "Contraception and Abortion in Roman Catholicism," in *Sacred Rights*, Maguire, ed., 71.

43. Quoted in David Orr, "For the Love of Life," *Conservation Biology* 6, no. 4 (December 1992), 486.

44. Wendell Berry, *Sex, Economy, Freedom, and Community* (New York: Pantheon, 1993), 114.

April 2016
Half Price Books
St. Paul
$2⁰⁰